PROFESSORS ARE FROM MARS®,
STUDENTS ARE FROM SNICKERS®

PROFESSORS ARE FROM MARS®, STUDENTS ARE FROM SNICKERS®

How to Write and Deliver Humor in the Classroom and in Professional Presentations

Ronald A. Berk

STERLING, VIRGINIA

First published by Stylus Publishing, LLC, 2003

Stylus Publishing, LLC
22883 Quicksilver Drive
Sterling, Virginia 20166

Originally published by Mendota Press, an
imprint of Magna Publications, Inc., 1998
Copyright © 2003 by Stylus Publishing, LLC

**Library of Congress
Cataloging-in-Publication Data**

Berk, Ronald A.
    Professors are from Mars, students are from
        Snickers : how to write and deliver humor
        in the classroom and in professional
        presentations / Ronald A. Berk.
            p. cm.
    Includes bibliographical references and index.
    ISBN 1-57922-070-3 (alk. paper)
    1. Humor in education. 2. College teaching.
    I. Title.

LB2326.B47 2003
378.1'2—dc21
                                        2003042368

First edition, 1998. Reprinted by Stylus
Publishing, LLC, 2003
ISBN: paperback 1-57922-070-3

Printed in the United States of America
All first editions printed on acid free paper

Acknowledgements

I give gigantic thank you's to gifted communicator Joe Stowell, my esteemed role model, who has been a constant source of inspiration and guidance, and to jocular Jim Popham, my mirthful mentor, whose supportiveness in all of my efforts to teach and write humorously, especially this book, has meant so much. I express my sincere appreciation to the American Educational Research Association's Professional Development and Training Committee and to Milt Cox, Director of the Lilly Conference on College Teaching, for taking risks by accepting my proposals to conduct training sessions on humor for professors. The success of those sessions was a primary stimulant for writing this book. I also thank Bill Gorth, Paula Nassif, Dick Allen, Barbara Appel, and Liz Pisarczyk for encouraging my use of humor in formal research presentations at National Evaluation Systems Conferences and actually publishing the humor in the proceedings.

I am grateful for the valuable suggestions and encouragement from Bill Russell, Bob Brennan, John Fremer, Jim Impara, and Barbara Plake, and for the special patience and humor support by Ada Davis, Kate Lears, Maureen Maguire, Jane Fall-Dickson, and Sheila Xu. Everyone who read a draft of the manuscript agreed unanimously that it was marginally creative, except for one tiny flaw: "It's the stupidest thing you've ever written." A few of the more heartwarming and inspiring reactions are listed below:

- "I'd rather endure the pain of a kidney stone the size of the Epcot golf ball than be forced to read this book again."
- "The usefulness of the information provided is below slime and slightly above sludge."
- "Reading the text is like watching the 'Running of the Bulls,' only less organized."
- "Humor? What humor? I didn't see any. Your feeble attempts at being funny are definitely an acquired taste, at best. Yuk. Yuk."
- "After reading this, I now have a clear picture of why your students see you as a middle-aged piñata."
- "The book is professional suicide. You don't need Kevorkian."
- "We now have further concrete evidence on how a mind is a terrible thing to waste."
- "No wonder your students are comatose by the end of your classes."
- "It made me laugh so hard that my dry lips cracked and my gums bled profusely."

I also acknowledge Mendota Press for taking a chance on this book project and for their commitment to quality publishing. I am especially grateful to my two editors: first, Ken Zielske, for his guidance and patience, although I burned him out within the first few months, and second, Judith Clayton, whose sensitivity and diplomatic and editorial skills are reflected in these inspiring words: "Ron, this book better be funny and make us buckets of money." (Just kidding. She really didn't say that. She actually said "dumpsters of money.") Judith was the best editor with whom any author could work.

For your added amusement and to keep you awake in between all of the boring stuff, every flub, blunder, gaffe, and typographical error is intentional. I thank my administrative secretary, Ellen Spies, for not correcting these nonerrors and for word processing everything else.

Finally, I want to thank my family who have always known I was totally nuts, particularly my wife, Marion, and my two daughters, Corinne and Marissa, who, I am proud to say, are chips off the old twisted block.

Research Funding Sources: The two days of research necessary to throw this book together was generously funded by the following institutions:

Moisha & Izzy's Bagel Shop

Beenie Weenie's Carpet Cleaning

Bubba's Bar-B-Que and Bullwhip Shop

National Society for the Prevention of Cruelty to Professors Who Mean Well but Are Just Dull

Dedications

To my mother, who taught me the value of a sense of humor

To all of those professors from Mars, without whose seriousness about everything there would be no need for this book

To all of my students from Snickers, without whose reinforcement of my jocular efforts I wouldn't be completely out of control today

Table of Contents

Introduction

According to my most recent super-precise, rounding-to-the-sixth-decimal-point calculations, there are a gazillion joke and humor books on every conceivable subject in the marketplace. In fact, some of them are, like, too totally weird to describe. Let's just say the excessive use of talcum powder combined with barnyard animals can yield really scuzzy jokes. Despite all of the humor books, there are only a handful of "how to" books that proffer step-by-step procedures for writing and presenting humor (Blumenfeld & Alpern, 1994; Iapoce, 1988; Wright & Wright, 1985). Some in the public speaking and communication literature contain a chapter on using humor in formal speeches (Allen, 1986; Davis, 1991; Detz, 1992; Hoff, 1992). There are also a few volumes on comedy writing and stand-up comedy methods (Allen, 1987; Carter, 1989; Helitzer, 1993; Perret, 1982a, 1982b, 1990, 1993), plus one on producing mirthful responses by smashing ordinary household appliances and food to smithereens (Gallagher, 1997).

At present there is nothing in print, electronic, or paranormal form that applies humor to academia. There are no guidelines or "how to" material anywhere on this planet that provide a step-by-step approach to writing humorous material, applying it to academic disciplines, and delivering it effectively in college classrooms and professional presentations. Although numerous generic techniques can be drawn from existing sources and used in any presentation, there is potentially a wealth of humorous material and an assortment of strategies unique to university teaching and research that have never been systematically explored or tested; that is, until now. This book tackles those tasks by dredging up jocular gems from the bowels (a.k.a. sanctum sanctora) of contemporary institutions of higher education or, in intergalactic terms, "boldly goes where no professor has gone before!"

Unlike the books on comedy writing, this one is not the least bit funny and it emphasizes "low-risk" humor strategies that can be planned and integrated into instruction to facilitate learning. In other words, humor is conceptualized and employed as a legitimate teaching tool rather than as only the typical "high-risk" stand-up joke or ad-lib in response to a student's question. Humor is used to break down barriers to communication so that professors can better connect and deliver their messages to students and other audiences. The humor methods are consistent with the latest cutting-edge college teaching techniques, such as inactive learning, uncooperative and noncollaborative learning, non-critical thinking, and low-tech unmediated instruction. Further, several of the methods recommended for oral presentations are extended to different types of written material: (a) professional publications, such as journal articles, chapters, books, subpoenas, and NCAA violations, (b) forms of communication, such as memos, e-mail, faxes, letters of resignation, Post-its, and paper airplanes, and (c) other academic documents, such as meeting agendas and minutes, bylaws, theater tickets, pink slips, and doodles.

This volume was thrown together hastily, the product of the three random, interrelated historical events: (1) my scary experimentation and experiences with a variety of humor techniques and material in my own undergraduate and graduate classes and keynote and research presentations over the past decade; (2) my questionable research on the effectiveness of each humor strategy and the composite impact of several strategies on changing attitudes, anxiety, and achievement; and (3) the jocular training sessions/courses I have conducted at national teaching and research conferences and university faculty development symposia for professors from the most remote crevices in the universe, such as Snow Shovel, Minnesota; Buffalo Wings, Wyoming; Mosquito Repellent, Florida; and Armadillo, Texas.

It should be evident by now that as a professor, I take humor very seriously; it's no laughing matter. This book on humor is written for professors, trainers, researchers, and administrators who work in any institution of higher education or research, such as specialized research/training institutes or corporations, community colleges, four-year colleges, and universities. If you teach, train, and/or deliver presentations of any kind to any audience in any of those settings, fancy hotels, or on mountaintops, then you should find this book useful. Even professionals in nonacademic environments who must present frequently to their peers or lay audiences may see value in the techniques. These persons may include physicians, nurses, and other healthcare personnel, corporate trainers, managers, and executives, government administrators, religious leaders, politicians, weedwacker repair guys, fishing lure salespersons, and just about anyone else with a pulse. The methods described in the following chapters are applicable to any discipline, content area, or ice cold beverage.

The purpose of this guidebook is to present a wide array of techniques from which you can select those that best fit: (a) your personality and teaching or presentation style, (b) the subject matter you teach or present, (c) your audience, and (d) your eating habits. The material is designed to meet the needs of the "humor challenged" or "jocularly arthritic" professional* who has never tried to use humor or is now hesitant to attempt it because of previous negative experiences (a.k.a. "bombs"), the jocular veteran who incorporates humor regularly into his or her presentations, and everyone else between those two extremes, from no use to regular use.

At this point, you should stop and ask yourself, "Where do I fall on this humor use continuum, pray tell?" If you don't fall anywhere on that continuum, find yourself another continuum. Face it, you're an outlier. You might attempt to get a refund for this book, but you probably won't because I already see a coffee cup ring on this page. If you do fall on the humor use continuum, it is hoped that this guide will supply you with techniques to develop, improve, or sharpen your humor writing skills and delivery. It should also expand your available choices of humor tools by furnishing ready-to-use copyrighted material that can be stolen as is or modified for your own purposes. The pool of my material combined with yours should permit you to inject humor into your presentations at every appropriate and inappropriate opportunity.

I suggest that you read the first five chapters in sequence to build your fundamental skills for writing and delivery. You may then continue to Chapter 6 for specific classroom strategies, go to Chapter 7 on professional presentations based on your own needs, or completely ignore these suggestions and skip all over the book, which is more fun anyway. Reading, however, is only the first step. It is not expected that reading alone will be sufficient to attain your humor goals, whatever they are. You must read with a companion: animal, vegetable, mineral, or The Club. More than that, you must do it. "What is *it?*" you query. Use the techniques and examples to generate your own material and execute the step-by-step procedures to deliver your material in your

---

Note: This book is *closed-captioned for the Humor-Impaired.* Since Dave Barry (1991, p. 12) introduced this "groundbreaking" idea in one of his columns, it seemed appropriate to apply it to this book. After each attempted joke, the humor element will be explained in ( ) so that those of you who are Humor-Impaired can laugh along with the rest of us.

classes and presentations. Chapter 8 is included for those of you who would like to extend that material to your publications and academic communications and documents, which can potentially get you into more trouble than all of the preceding methods combined.

Only through continuous practice and an accumulation of experience in writing and performing humorous material can you realistically expect to be successful. Professionals in the performing arts, sports, and gardening practice their craft every day in preparation for those special occasions when it counts the most, whether they're musicians, singers, dancers, actors, comedians, athletes, or Martha Stewart. Without practice, your humor skills can become dull, rusty, corroded, and infected. It is essential that you constantly fine tune your natural or acquired humor skills and learn new ones to keep your humor fresh, appropriate, and effective. The best part of all of this practice is that it's FUN! In nearly 25 years of university teaching, I have never had so much fun and laughed so much as I have in the past few years, and my students seem to be learning more because of it rather than in spite of it. Some of us rarely succeed at anything unless we have fun doing it. As two of America's greatest philosophers, Ben & Jerry, once said, "If it's not fun, why do it?" I challenge you to do the same.

Chapter 1

Why Use Humor?

Ned Rorem has defined humor as "the ability to see three sides of one coin." The humorist sees the third side, something that most people don't see. Norman Cousins says, "True humor is a sort of train wreck of the mind. You're going along a track and there's a sudden collapse of logic, the cars go off the track, and then they pile up and build into laughter." Ken Davis (1991) has suggested that it helps to have a "twisted mind" to notice the humorous element in a given situation. There are probably at least another 500 definitions, concepts, notions, and interpretations of humor and laughter (Goodman, 1995).

The key question is why use humor as a teaching tool in our classrooms and professional presentations? As academicians, I bet a few of you are probably thinking, "If you're asking me to seriously consider humor, which could radically alter my proven time-tested approach to teaching, known technically as the Non-Critical-Thinking-Passive-Comatose-Boring Method, show me the hard evidence that it works." The bottom line, after all, is to increase learning. "Well, where's the evidence?" I don't have a clue! (Just kidding.)

I wish I could cite a humongous corpus (a constellation better known as the Big Belly) of research that would satisfy your empirical pangs. It simply doesn't exist. There are a jillion studies that have examined the effects of laughter on our mind and body, but very few that have explored the use of humor to facilitate learning in the college classroom.

A brief journey through the literature is presented next. Let's begin this bumpy ride with an autopsy of laughter.

Josh Billings, a 19th century humorist, said, "Anatomically considered, laughing is a sensation of feeling good all over and allowing it principally in one spot . . . Genuine laughing is a vent of the soul, the nostrils of the heart, and it is just as necessary for health and happiness as spring water is for a trout" (Flynn, 1960, p.43). Kuhn (1994) has partitioned laughter into 15 stages:

1. SMIRK: Slight, often fleeting upturning of the corners of the mouth, completely voluntary and controllable.

2. SMILE: Silent, voluntary and controllable, more perceptible than a smirk; begins to release endorphins.

3. GRIN: Silent, controllable, but uses more facial muscles (e.g., eyes begin to narrow).

4. SNICKER: First emergence of sound with facial muscles, but still controllable (if you hold in a snicker, it builds up gas).

5. GIGGLE: Has a 50% chance of reversal to avoid a full laugh; sound of giggling is amusing; efforts to suppress it tend to increase its strength.

6. CHUCKLE: Involves chest muscles with deeper pitch.

7. CHORTLE: Originates even deeper in chest and involves muscles of torso; usually provokes laughter in others.

8. LAUGH: Involves facial and thoracic muscles as well as abdomen and extremities; sound of barking or snorting.

9. CACKLE: First involuntary stage; pitch is higher and body begins to rock, spine extends and flexes, with an upturning of head.

10. GUFFAW: Full body response; feet stomp, arms wave, thighs are slapped, torso rocks, sound is deep and loud; may result in free flowing of tears, increased heart rate, and breathlessness; strongest solitary laughter experience.

11. HOWL: Volume and pitch rise higher and higher and body becomes more animated.

12. SHRIEK: Greater intensity than howl; sense of helplessness and vulnerability.

13. ROAR: Lose individuality; audience roars!

14. CONVULSE: Body is completely out of control in a "fit" of laughter resembling a seizure; extremities flail aimlessly, balance is lost, listener gasps for breath, collapses or falls off chair.

15. DIES LAUGHING: Instant of total helplessness; a brief, physically intense, transcendent experience; having died, we are

thereafter "reborn" in a refreshing moment of breathlessness and exhaustion with colors more vivid and everything sparkling; everything is renewed. (Adapted from pp. 13–15).

Given these psychological and physiological effects of laughing, it is not recommended that you stifle or try to suppress your laughter internally. Fred Allen once warned, if you do, "it goes back down and spreads to your hips."

> **WARNING:** Reading the following paragraphs, which contain a drillion killion research findings and citations, could cause drowsiness, nausea, bloating, numbness, various mutations, and a substantial penalty for early withdrawal. I know you're thinking, "Why not just whack me in both kneecaps with a sledge hammer!" Cruel? Sick? Inhumane? Perhaps. But I couldn't help it. My name is Ron and I'm a professoroholic.

Mounting evidence on the psychological effects of laughter indicates that it can decrease anxiety and stress, improve self-esteem, and increase motivation and perceived quality of life (Berk et al., 1989b; Cornett, 1986; Cousins, 1989; Fry, 1992; Martin & Dobbin, 1988; Martin & Lefcourt, 1983). There is also a smidgen (about two tablespoons) of evidence that it can decrease whining, howling, bickering, and body-piercing (Personal communication with Dionne Warwick, July 1997). Several measures of "sense of humor," in fact, have been developed for use in this research, including the *Situational Humor Response Questionnaire* (Martin & Lefcourt, 1984), *Coping Humor Scale* (Martin & Lefcourt, 1983), *Sense of Humor Questionnaire* (Martin & Lefcourt, 1983; Svebak, 1974), and the *Jocular Scale of Whimsical Frivolity* (Berko & Bonzo, 1996).

Physiological benefits of laughter (a.k.a. mirthful responses) have been found for the muscular, respiratory, cardiovascular, endocrine, immune, and central nervous systems (Fry, 1986, 1992). Its effects on some "other" systems are too gross to mention. (Hint: They involve slimy goop and rutabagas.) The specific physiological effects include the following: (a) relaxes muscles (Fry, 1992; Paskind, 1932), (b) stimulates circulation (Fry & Savin, 1988; Fry & Stoft, 1971), (c) improves respiration and exercises the lungs and chest muscles (Fry & Rader, 1977; Lloyd, 1938), (d) decreases serum cortisol, dopec, and epinephrine levels in the blood (Berk et al., 1988; Berk, Tan, Napier, & Eby, 1989a; Fry, 1971, 1984a, 1992), (e) increases immune system's ability to respond and protect us (Berk et al., 1989a; Dillon, Minchoff, & Baker, 1985; Martin & Dobbin, 1988), (f) increases the production of endorphins that decrease pain (Berk et al., 1989b), (g) lowers pulse rate and blood pressure (Fry & Savin, 1988), and (h) relieves hemorrhoids, psoriasis, gangrene, projectile vomiting, gingivitis, and anthrax (Greene,

Benton, Carter, & Ross, 1997). Considering these effects, do you now wonder why we feel so good, even euphoric, after a good laugh? "No," you say. Uh. Like you're not supposed to answer my rhetorical questions. I guess you were confused by the question mark at the end. Sorry.

For those of you who don't like to exercise, laughter should be an extremely tempting alternative. Norman Cousins has stated that "Laughter is a form of jogging for the innards." You can produce endorphins without getting off your keester or putting down the remote. Unfortunately, its aerobic value is limited, unless of course you engage in convulsive laughter (see stage 14) for sustained periods of 20 to 30 minutes at least three times a week. Instead of hopping on your treadmill, stairmaster, pommel horse, or mechanical bull and watching Richard Simmons sweat his guts out, flip on *Comedy Central* or your favorite hysterical video and laugh yourself silly while your innards have a seizure. Give it a whirl and let me know whether you experience a "jocular high."

The research generated on the effects of humor on college teaching is scientifically less rigorous than in the previous research domain. Much of it is anecdotal, uncontrolled, pre-experimental, correlational, metaphysical, transcendental, extraterrestrial, and inorganic. The use of humor as a teaching tool in college classrooms rarely has been implemented systematically. It is frequently a random act that occurs spontaneously (Bryant, Crane, Comisky & Zillmann, 1980a) rather than intentionally to achieve specific learning outcomes. The research evidence stockpiled over the past 30 years is sparse, inconclusive (Gruner, 1967, 1970; Powell & Andresen, 1985; Taylor, 1964), contradictory (Bryant, Comisky & Zillmann, 1979; Kaplan & Pascoe, 1977; Smith, Ascough, Ettinger, & Nelson, 1971), and rather putrid after all of that time without refrigeration.

A few studies have examined the use of humor in introductory textbooks in psychology (Browning, 1977) and communication (Bryant, Gula, & Zillmann, 1980b) and humorous illustrations in communication texts (Bryant, Brown, Silberberg, & Elliott, 1981; Klein, Bryant & Zillmann, 1982). However, there are numerous and typically unsubstantiated Swine flu*-like claims about the benefits of humor in college teaching contaminating the literature: (a) decreases anxiety, tension, stress, and boredom; (b) improves attitudes toward the subject; (c) increases comprehension, cognitive retention, interest, and task performance; (d) increases motivation to learn and satisfaction with learning; and (e) promotes creativity and divergent thinking (Adams, 1974; Berk, 1997a; Berk & Nanda, 1997; Bryant et al., 1980a; Darling & Civikly, 1987; Edwards & Gibboney, 1992; Elmore & Pohlmann, 1978; Fry, 1984b; Hashem, 1994; Kaplan & Pascoe, 1977; Korobkin, 1988; Moses & Friedman, 1986; Parrott, 1994; Powell & Andresen, 1985;

---

*Remember, that was the epidemic that had to be canceled due to lack of germs!

Smith et al., 1971; Watson & Emerson, 1988; Welker, 1977; Zillmann & Bryant, 1983).

In the literature on humor, it is possible to find several lists of advantages of using humor to communicate effectively. For example, the Wright brothers, Wright and Wright (1985), present the following:

1. It is one of the most effective forms of emotional communication;
2. It can dissolve tension in people to whom you are relating and can help them relax;
3. It can help you gain and keep your listeners' attention;
4. It can increase your credibility and help you come across as a real person;
5. It can help overcome resistance to points you are trying to make;
6. It can provide needed breaks in a... speech; and
7. It can help drive home a point. (pp. 21–22)

Applying humor to the broader contexts of work and life, Blumenfeld and Alpern (1994) identified 12 benefits:

1. Humor makes work fun;
2. Humor can help us cope with problems;
3. Humor with a hint of playfulness is a safety valve for aggression and an acceptable means to express anger;
4. Humor offers perspective and balance;
5. Humor isn't fattening.
6. Humor is a means of communication and creative expression;
7. Humor provides temporary relief from society's restrictive regulations;
8. Humor is a way to express the truth even when truth is feared and repressed;
9. Humor is mentally and physically good for you;
10. Laughter affirms life and brings people together;
11. Humor often succeeds where other methods have failed; and
12. It beats all the alternatives. (pp. 8–9)

So what can be concluded from the preceding mixture of evidence on the value of humor? Not a lot. First, there is no solid empirical foundation (a.k.a. nothing concrete, not even gravel) to link humor to college students' attitudes and performance. The variety of types and forms of humor that can be systematically integrated into instruction and professional presentations has not been fully explored and evaluated. Previous research has not investigated the effectiveness of "low-risk" versus "high-risk" humor, oral versus written formats, content-specific versus generic humor, clean versus dirty humor, Laverne versus Shirley, and Siegfried versus Roy. Further, no one has tested techniques for inserting humor into traditional lecture content and standard print material other than textbooks, such as syllabi, handouts, assignments, homework problems, project outlines, exams, menus, job applications, and parking tickets. Second, the paucity of studies in humor research does not provide evidence to substantiate many of the claimed advantages of using humor or Pop Tarts.

However, despite these deficiencies in the research, the psychological and physiological effects of laughter, which, as you remember, you really liked, combined with the experience in using humor to improve communication, indicate there is value and several potential benefits to be gained from applying humor as a teaching tool, plus I needed some atom of legitimacy to justify writing this book. Building on this research and experiential foundation, the techniques presented in this book were derived from the ideas found in the literature on public speaking (Allen, 1986; Detz, 1992; Ehrlich, 1992; Filson, 1991; Flacks & Raspberry, 1982; Hoff, 1992; Montgomery, 1979), communication (Booher, 1994; Davis, 1991; Hamlin, 1988; Sigband & Bell, 1994), humor and stand-up comedy (Allen, 1987; Blumenfeld & Alpern, 1994; Carter, 1989; Helitzer, 1993; Iapoce, 1988; Perret, 1982a, 1982b, 1990, 1993, Wright & Wright, 1985), and Tony Robbins' get-rich-quick schemes. In addition, a few of the strategies proposed have been adapted from those employed by motivational speakers, such as Ernest Borgnine and Miss Piggy. I also borrowed ideas from religious leaders I have observed, although I forgot to return them. All of the other strategies I either spotted on Doppler radar or I simply made up, the products of a twisted sense of reality and my progressive mental deterioration.

Chapter 2

Anatomy of Humor

Humor has been defined by Steven Leacock as "the kindly contempla-
tion of the incongruities of life and the artistic expression thereof."
Most any form of humor must have INCONGRUITY, the *juxtaposition
of the expected with the unexpected.* "Incongruity" is derived from two Latin
root words: "in," meaning "to produce," and "congruitus," meaning,
"uncontrolled laughter with occasional snorts." The unexpected component must be illogical, exaggerated, unreasonable, inappropriate, or
just plain weird. The sharper the incongruity and the more suddenly it
can be introduced, the more certain the laugh and the louder and
longer it will be (Asimov, 1971). In other words, "pump irony." The
more extreme, absurd, and bizarre the twist, the more effective the
humor. The unexpected twist, commonly referred to as the "punch
line," typically occurs at the end of the humor, whether it is a top 10
list, a one-liner, an anecdote, or one of my sentences.

The basic structure for humorous material consists of three elements: (1) a commonly understood situation, (2) a build-up of tension,
and (3) the unexpected twist or punch line. This structure applies to
virtually all forms of humor, and it may take a thousand and one forms.
As Steve Allen (1987) noted, "It isn't even always funny, because what
is funny is a matter of personal opinion" (p. x). One of the great critical thinkers of our time, Dave Barry (1988), said, "What may seem

depressing or even tragic to one person may seem like an absolute scream to another person" (p. 1).

Commonly Understood Situation

The first element in humor is a situation that is commonly understood and to which everyone in the audience can relate. Some of the best humor has to do with ordinary situations with which we're all familiar, such as jousting, cleaning a shotgun, snowboarding, and parachuting onto the point of the Seattle Space Needle (Ouch!). It is the "expected" or familiar part of the humor that provides the premise or lead-in for the other two elements. As the springboard for a joke, the expected element is essential to create the proper mood for the build-up of tension and introduction of the humorous twist. If the audience doesn't understand or is unfamiliar with the premise (assuming they don't have the collective intelligence of an avocado), the tension will not build and the punch in the punch line is removed. What remains is just a flat line, like the one on the cardiac monitor, and you know what that means. Instead of the tension exploding, it simple fizzles and you croak. Probably most of us have told jokes in our classes that bombed because our students didn't understand the first element and we suspected they didn't "get" the punch line. It is essential that this first element is appropriate for our audience, whether it's the students in our class or researchers at a conference.

This initial criterion must be met for generic humor which may be applicable to a variety of audiences as well as for content-specific professional humor or "in-jokes." For example, the following list of "twisted" familiar expressions would be understood by students, academicians in any discipline, and lay people:

- Where there's a will, there's a won't.
- To err is human, but it feels divine.
- Cleanliness is next to impossible.
- Beauty is only surgery deep.

Rodney Dangerfield has tons of one-liners to which everyone can relate, such as the following:

- When I was a kid, we were so poor I got batteries—toys not included.
- I was such an ugly kid, my mother got morning sickness after I was born.

In contrast to these examples is professional humor that only your students or academicians might understand and appreciate. For example, the following multiple-choice items relate to university classes, research, and professional tests:

- As a professor, which one of the following is a sign you're NOT going to have a good day?

  A. As you enter your classroom, all of the students raise knives above their heads and hum the shower music from *Psycho*

  B. During one of your best lectures, a dozen students drift into a coma and the rest scurry to complete their living wills

  C. After you pass back midterm exams, you notice a line forming outside of your office the length of the Great Wall of Hong Kong

  D. When you ask a student who failed your exam, "Do you feel you did your best?" The student responds, "Bite Me!"

or

- Based on our experience in submitting manuscripts to the Journal of (insert name of your journal), what RESEARCH ERROR is a sure-fire reason for rejection?

  A. You assigned participants to treatment groups using the "eenie meenie meinie moe" method.

  B. You administered a self-esteem scale to the subjects that was normed on serial killers at San Quentin.

  C. You claimed statistically significant results at the .06 rather than .05 level.

  D. You rounded off all of your correlation coefficients to the nearest whole number, such as 1.

or

- What is the BEST "hint" for preparing to take a professional licensing or certification test?

  A. Block out all of your professional experiences and knowledge from articles and books you may have read; instead, concentrate on your vacation fantasies.

  B. Eat a hearty breakfast, such as a three-egg ranch omelette, steak, bacon, sausage, hashbrowns, and a liter of coffee.

  C. Take your mutilated admission ticket, borrowed driver's license, and one dull no. 3 pencil without an eraser to the test center.

  D. Set your alarm to get up five minutes before the exam begins and don't look at the directions to the test center until you're in your car.

  E. Open the "Preparation Manual" for the first time while driving to the test center, and glance at the sample items during stop lights.

The following top 10 list could be presented to any class:

Top 10 List of Ways You Can Become
Unpopular With Your Classmates

10. Make promises you can't possibly keep.

9. Convince classmates to take risks you wouldn't touch.

8. Say the coffee is decaf when it isn't.

7. Don't show up after you offer a classmate a lift.

6. Never acknowledge anyone else's contribution to anything.

5. Ask classmates how they're doing, but don't wait for a response.

4. When giving a classmate directions to a favorite downtown hot spot, leave out a turn or two.

3. In the lab, put things back where they don't belong.

2. Borrow a classmate's notes and then lose them.

And the number 1 way you can become unpopular with your classmates:

1. Ask classmates who don't like you for help.

Humor that pokes fun at memos, committees, meetings, and practices in our profession would have a special meaning to faculty and administrators. For example:

• There is an UNWRITTEN law in my department: Everyone has to write memos, but no one has to read them. If it were a WRITTEN law, it would be a memo; then no one would find out about it!

or

• Which one of the following MOST accurately characterizes a COMMITTEE at your institution?

A. A committee is the only group structure capable of reproducing itself in the form of baby subcommittees.

B. A committee is the only life form with 10 stomachs and no brain.

C. A committee is the only entity that keeps on going, and going, and going (other than the Energizer Bunny).

D. A committee is a mechanism for producing reports with recommendations, which almost guarantees no one will implement.

E. A committee is a dark back alley down which creative ideas are lured and then quietly strangled.

or

- According to "Murphy's Laws," what's the most important lesson we've learned from our research?

    A. If you set the minimum level of performance as a standard, it soon becomes the maximum.

    B. If it's worth doing, it's worth overdoing.

    C. For every vision, there's an equal and opposite revision.

    D. A simple problem can be made insoluble if enough meetings are held to discuss it.

Build-Up of Tension

The second element is the build-up of tension. Now I bet you're thinking, "That's just what my students need. More tension." Trust me on this one. This tension will be good for them, plus they'll get to release it. After all the chapters you've known me, have I ever given you a bum steer, or even a water buffalo? I think it's time to get back to the topic of this paragraph. This build-up of tension is a function of the length of the humorous material up to the punch line. In an anecdote, there is time to build tension as the story unfolds and details are revealed. For example:

> I have no illusion that attending my classes is essential to get "A's" in this course. I recall the story of a student who attended just the first class of the semester and did not show up again until the final exam. He scored 95% on the exam. The professor was shocked because she knew he hadn't come to class all semester. She wrote "see me" on the cover of the exam. After the exams were passed back and the class was over, the student approached the professor and said, "You wanted to see me about my exam?" The professor responded, "Yes. How did you get a 95 on that exam?" The student answered, "Well, it would have been 100, but I went to your first class and got confused."

Tension is building throughout the story and increases markedly as the punch line is anticipated when the student answers the professor, "Well, it would have been 100..."

In contrast to this gradual build-up of tension is the one-liner which builds very quickly within the first part of the statement. For example:

> The shortest distance between 2 points is usually *under construction.*

Here everything in the line except the punch (shown in italics) is used to build tension, plus it is the beginning of an expression with which everyone is familiar. There must be a slight pause after "usually," before delivering the punch. Timing is critical to the success of a one-liner. If it bombs, your students are stuck with a lot of built-up tension. This tension should not be allowed to increase and fester. "Why?" you ask. Festering tension can smart, like being poked in the eyeballs by one of the Three Stooges, and if it is not released by laughing, your students will release it after class by beating you senseless with sticks.

A variation on the one-liner is the one- or two-line *non sequitur* (Latin, meaning literally, "not on my furniture you don't"). It is defined as "a kind of joke in which the punch line seems to have nothing to do with the narrative content of the joke proper" (Charney, 1995, p. 339). The *non sequitur* is at the heart of Woody Allen's humor (1971, 1975, 1980). Charney's (1995) analysis of Allen's work suggests "we laugh at the yoking of what seem like totally disparate ideas" (p. 341). Here are a few examples:

- The universe is merely a fleeting idea in God's mind — a pretty uncomfortable thought, particularly if you've just made a down payment on a house. (Allen, 1971, p. 25)

- What if everything is an illusion and nothing exists? In that case, I definitely overpaid for my carpet. (Allen, 1975, p. 6)

- An inhabited planet named Quelm so distant from the earth that man traveling at the speed of light would take six million years to get there, although they are planning an express route that will cut two hours off the trip. (Allen, 1975, p. 183)

- In addition to these obstacles on Quelm, there is no oxygen to support life as we know it, and what creatures do exist find it hard to earn a living without holding down two jobs. (Allen, 1975, pp. 183-184)

The humor formula can be extended to multiple-choice format items where the stem builds tension and the three to five choices are basically one-liners, each with its own punch. Further, the choices build tension for the last and, hopefully, best one-liner in the last choice. This format appears frequently in humor books and is used by David Letterman in his "person-in-the-street" gags. The one-liner choices in the following example have been adapted from Andrews (1994).

Which one of the following behaviors suggest your gray cells have gone on sabbatical (or you're beginning to lose it!)?

A. You use a match to see better when looking for a gas leak in your house.

B. You buy your kid a pet because he or she promises to take care of it.

C. You advise your teenager to use his or her own best judgment.

D. You anger your proctologist just before your exam.

This same formula is used for top 10 lists. In fact, the preceding multiple-choice format is essentially a top 4 list. If 6 of the 10 one-liners bomb in your top 10 list, you have three choices: (a) continue to use your "mediocre" top 10 list, (b) pick the 4 or 5 winning one-liners and reformat them as a "dynamite" multiple-choice item, or (c) pack your bags and move to Mr. Potato Head, Idaho. For the top 10 format, the title plays the role of the stem in the multiple-choice item and the one-liners build the tension toward the final one-liner — "And the number one sign your gray cells have gone on sabbatical . . ." Here is the original top 10 version (adapted from Andrews, 1994) of the preceding multiple-choice item:

Top 10 Signs Your Gray Cells Have Gone on Sabbatical

10. You use a match to see better when looking for a gas leak in your house.
9. You lend money to a relative and say, "Pay me back when you can."
8. You write down "poet" as your last job on a job application.
7. You try to analyze your relationship with your significant other.
6. You buy a kid a pet because he or she promises to take care of it.
5. You anger your proctologist just before your exam.
4. You advise a teenager to use his or her own best judgment.
3. You take a job as an earthquake insurance salesperson in California.
2. You marry a really good divorce lawyer.
1. You read Russian literature when you're depressed.

Unexpected Twist

The final element in humor is the sudden and unexpected twist, the quick flip from sense to no-sense. It triggers the laughter by providing the audience with the opportunity to release their tension built-up by the first two elements. The incongruity between the "expected" (elements 1 and 2) and "unexpected" (element 3) was illustrated in each of the preceding examples. The story is probably the longest form of this incongruity and the shortest is two words, as in an oxymoron, such as "JUMBO shrimp" or "hospital food."

As mentioned previously, the sharper the contrast and the more sudden it strikes you, the more successful the humor. Achieving this goal requires the most concentrated levels of creativity, imagination, twistedness, and controlled substances. The "punch" in any form of humor is where the rubber meets the Budweiser frog. Squish. This third element is the most difficult to write and to deliver. No pressure, huh? Chapters 3 and 5 will guide you through those processes, respectively.

Structural Variations

I frequently use different test item formats to illustrate strategies for measuring the performance of teachers, students, and administrators, and employees who take licensing and certification tests. These formats are taught in my classes and also presented to non-technically trained professional audiences. The various item formats furnish the formats for the items and generic content provides the humor. A few are shown below. Inspect each format to identify the three elements described previously. The punch line is identified in italics for each item.

Complex Multiple-Choice

Which of the following signs suggest you're NOT YOUNG anymore?

(a) You enter a room and *totally forget what you went in for.*

(b) You experience irregularity with *greater regularity.*

(c) Getting the mail is one of the *highlights of your day.*

(d) You've got antacids *stashed all over the house.*

(e) You go from being a do-it-yourselfer *to a hire-someone-elser.*

A. (a) and (b)

B. (a) and (e)

C. (b), (c), and (d)

D. (b), (d), and (e)

   This item follows the same structure as the standard multiple-choice item, except the actual answer choices are combinations of the primary choices listed first. The humor is injected into the stem and five primary choices only. The content in the stem and choices represents commonly understood behaviors for audiences in the 30 to infinity age range. Certainly, the older you are, the more you can relate to the choices. The stem builds the tension at first by setting a funny premise. The green light is on for "Here comes the joke." Each choice is a one-liner (adapted from those in McTigue, 1994) with the formula for the build-up of tension in the first part and the punch at the end. The first four choices, (a) through (d), also build tension for the final (e) one-liner, which is the punch line for the entire item.

Completion

1. Psychiatry is the care of the id by the (_odd_) .
2 Every morning is the dawn of a new (_error_) .
3. Nothing succeeds like (_recess_) . (Stanley Horowitz)

This series of examples of completion or fill-in-the-blank items are simply one-liners following the basic formula. The first element is a commonly understood term (item 1) or familiar saying (items 2 and 3) that builds the tension. The audience is expecting a different ending because of their familiarity with the first part of the expression. Obviously this item structure takes advantage of what the audience anticipates. We're playing with their minds. Further, the punch that finally comes at the end is just _one word,_ rather than the phrase format of the previous multiple-choice variation. This one-word punch creates a more sudden twist than the phrase, which is more gradual. It produces an unexpected shock to your psyche. This can have a stronger impact than the phrase and, consequently, may elicit more laughter.

Extended-Response Essay

1. Using the major economic theories of the 20th century, discuss the implications of the following quote:

   "Never try to keep up with the Joneses; _drag them down to your level._" (Quentin Crisp)

2. As a parent, describe the personal significance of the following recommendation:

   "Never raise your hand to your children; _it leaves your midsection unprotected._" (Robert Orben)

These examples demonstrate a combination of the approaches used in the preceding formats to produce the humor. The task or stimulus at the beginning of each essay presents a commonly understood, albeit serious, situation similar to the stem of the multiple-choice format. The second part of the item is just a one-liner quotation. The build-up of tension doesn't actually start until the first part of the quotation which, similar to completion item 3 above, is the beginning of a popular saying or expression, that is, another commonly understood situation. The twist in the second part is a completely unexpected ending to what the audience anticipates they know in the familiar expression. These "twisted" quotations can be very effective.

All of the preceding formats illustrate how the three elements of humor can be integrated through different structures. The notion of incongruity with both expected and unexpected components is present in these formats. You could probably generate a hundred variations of the three-prong formula demonstrated throughout this chapter. A variety of some of the most effective variations on this theme will be described in the next chapter. The essential rules for creating humor, however, do not change. They must exist in every form to produce laughter.

Chapter 3

Types and Forms of Humor

WARNING: The first section of this chapter on "high-risk" humor contains pretty serious stuff. However, it's just as important as the light-hearted fluff on "low-risk" humor that follows, though not nearly as important, as say, the Super Bowl or eating Brussels Sprouts (Yuck! Blecch!).

Although it was noted previously that humor can take on probably hundreds of forms, there are basically two major categories under which most forms can be lumped: high-risk and low-risk. Risk in this case relates to your chances of "bombing" or "dying" in front of an audience and the accompanying sense of embarrassment or humiliation. Since professors are not trained to be comedians, comedy writers, and actors, and very few may possess natural gifts for any of those professions, the issue of risk is pertinent. The goal of using humor in our classrooms and professional conferences is to maximize its benefits as a teaching tool and minimize its risks to our self-esteem and professional reputation.

High-Risk Humor

This type of humor is most easily illustrated by the stand-up comic. Jay Leno lives or dies on each joke and punch line. There is no doubt in the minds of the audience that they came to laugh and they expect Leno to deliver. That's his job. But it isn't ours. We don't have Leno's training and years of experience, yet when we tell a joke in our class or at a professorial meeting, somehow we expect uproarious laughter. Be realistic! Even a great joke can be botched by inept, lousy delivery. Delivering one-liners like Tim Allen or Jerry Seinfeld requires years of practice. (*Pop Quiz:* What is Tim Allen's middle name? *Hint:* It has "Tool" in it.)

We can learn to improve our delivery as well as our ability to write jokes or stories that are really funny. However, any joke or story that depends on a single punch line would be considered a high risk. There are volumes of joke books available everywhere to provide jokes for almost any occasion or situation, but I haven't found any that relate to college students, university life, or our responsibilities as professors. Maybe that will be the subject of my next book or, perhaps, yours.

Another form of high-risk humor is spontaneous humor or the "ad-lib" that is the witty response to some comment or situation. (We wish!) It is also the most frequently found form of humor in college classrooms based on a content analysis (Bryant et al., 1980a). (*Bonus Question:* What does "et al." mean? *Hint:* Wears a plaid flannel shirt and appears with Tim.) However, the spontaneous jocular thought that comes to mind expressed in the immediate response to a student's question can be dangerous. There are three risks: (1) the response isn't funny, (2) the humor is distracting, and/or (3) it offends someone.

First, "bombing" comes with the territory. You get accustomed to this outcome after a while. In fact, your recovery strategies tend to improve the more you "bomb." (A few appropriate strategies are suggested in Chapter 5.) Professional comedians such as Leno and Letterman bomb with some jokes every night. The risk is worth taking if that's the tone you have created in your class. Students expect you to joke and they want to laugh. Unfortunately, in spontaneous humor you can't expect to deliver a winner every time. However, the more risks I take, the better I get, and, the higher my hit rate over time.

Second, the humorous response may not relate to the educational point or to the content of the lecture. This can be very distracting to some students. One study by Bryant et al. (1980a) found that this risk is tolerated for male professors but not for female professors. That is, female professors whose humor was perceived as distracting to the educational message received exceptionally low scores on overall effectiveness. This evidence suggests that spontaneous humor should be pertinent to the educational content to be perceived by most students as part of effective teaching.

The third risk of offending someone is the most difficult to prevent and can produce the most serious consequences. Spontaneous humor is a split-second reaction and, as such, it is almost impossible to edit what comes out of our mouths so quickly. Humorous material that is developed in advance can be tested and edited to usually prevent any offensive content. The premise regarding the use of offensive humor is that any humor that could offend anyone in your classroom or audience is totally inappropriate. As professors, our role is completely different from the stand-up comic on *Comedy Central* who may tell jokes at the expense of his or her spouse, a politician, or a celebrity. If our raison d étre (a French expression meaning, "cinnamon-raisin bagel with cream cheese") is to be effective teachers, and the purpose of using humor is to better "connect" and "communicate" our message, an offensive comment in a joke can have the reverse effect. Instead of relaxing and opening up our students' minds to receive our message, they may cringe, tighten up, or withdraw mentally when something offensive is said. The humor has just backfired. Offensive humor shuts down communication and erects a barrier to learning. More will be said about this issue at the end of the chapter.

Low-Risk Humor

This type of humor reduces your chance of failure, while at the same time allowing you to build-up your risk-taking skills. There are a variety of formats that you can use as teaching tools to facilitate learning in your classroom or in professional presentations. They span a range of risks but, in general, are at the low end of the risk continuum. In this section, seven basic humor formats with a proven track record of funniness will be described and illustrated: (1) quotations and questions, (2) cartoons, (3) multiple-choice items, (4) top 10 lists, (5) anecdotes, (6) skits/dramatizations, and (7) ad-libs that aren't. Numerous other formats will be recommended in Chapters 6 and 7 that are specific to classroom and professional presentation applications, respectively.

Quotations and Questions. As mentioned in the previous chapter, a humorous quotation that may be a twist on a familiar saying is actually a one-liner. *Twisted well-known expressions* are widely used because everyone can relate to them and appreciate them. The incongruity from the expected to the unexpected is well-pronounced, strong, and sudden. The first part of the quotation is known to your audience, but the second part is not. It is that first part that can build the tension in the audience. They anticipate one serious ending and you zap them with an unexpected punch. Twisted popular expressions can be very effective.

Fortunately, with this format you have the option of delivering it orally like a stand-up comic or presenting it silently by having the audience do the work. Ripley himself might not believe this, but you do not have to say a word. The quote can be prepared on a colored overhead transparency or slide. Allowing a few moments for each person in the audience to read the quote can have a stronger impact than delivering it orally as a joke.

Here are examples of a few simple, well-known expressions that have been twisted. In fact, after reading these, you may want to put your own twist on others. Larsen (1995) has compiled hundreds of *Oddball Sayings, Witty Expressions, and Down Home Folklore* that need twisting. These one-liners may be presented singly or one at a time as part of a list:

- Many are called, but few are at home!
- Many are called, but few are called back!
- Where there's a will, there's a lawsuit. (Addison Mizner)
- Where there's a will, I want to be in it.
- In God we trust, all others need data.
- On a clear disk you can seek forever. (Virginia Beckwith)
- He or she who laughs last, thinks slowest. (Bob Lockhart)
- Beggars can't be on *Lifestyles of the Rich and Famous.*
- It doesn't matter whether you win or lose, just whether you beat the point spread. (Wally Juall)
- Change is inevitable, except from a vending machine.
- Don't look a gift horse in the patoot!
- Let a smile be your umbrella and you'll get a lot of rain in your face. (Tom Gill)
- If you step on a crack, you could break someone's habit.
- The grass is always greener when you use spray paint.
- People who live in glass houses are usually transparent.
- The way to a man's heart is through the plaque in his arteries.
- You can lead a horse to water, but you can't make him do a 2-1/2 flip in the pike position.
- Don't count your chickens before they cross the road. (Charles Belov)
- Sticks and stones may break my bones, but names involve my lawyer.
- A rolling stone gathers smashed objects in its path. (Margie Mereen)

- A closed mouth gathers no feet.
- People who make mountains out of molehills suffer from piles.

Another type of quotation is the *definition format*. A familiar term is simply given an absurd, bizarre, and, hopefully, funny definition. In this case, the definition is the punch. It doesn't permit the build-up of tension characterizing the twisted expression. However, it can still be quite effective if the definition is a play on words or part of a familiar saying that is outrageous or paints a humorous image in the minds of your audience. Strangely, graffiti is a major source for this type of quotation (see Frankel, Wilson, & Salo, 1996). For example:

- A team effort is a lot of people doing what I say.
- Diplomacy is the art of letting someone have your way.
- It's déjà vu all over again.
- Vu jà dé is the strange feeling that you've never been here before.
- A phoneless cord is for people who like peace and quiet.
- Familiarity breeds in tents.
- Pessimism means never having to be disappointed. (Thomas McKenna)
- "Shin" is a device for finding furniture in the dark.
- Abstinence makes the heart grow fonder. (Mark Miller)
- "Budget" is a systematic way to go broke.
- Reality is what refuses to go away when I stop believing in it.
- A conclusion is simply the point at which you got tired of thinking.

There are other quotations that may be just as funny as the preceding formats. However, they do not have the advantage of the sudden twist from something familiar to the unexpected punch. The impact may be different because the incongruity is not as strong or sharp. "Murphy's Laws" (Block, 1991) and graffiti (Frankel et al., 1996) usually fall into this quotation category. Here are several examples:

- If you look like your passport photo, you're too ill to travel. (Will Kommen)
- Bad spellers of the world, untie!
- Never get in a battle of wits without ammunition.
- TV enables you to be entertained in your home by people you wouldn't have in your home.
- The severity of the itch is inversely proportional to one's reach.
- Today's gifts are tomorrow's garage sales.
- When you go into court, you are putting your fate into the hands of 12 people who weren't smart enough to get out of jury duty. (Norm Crosby)

- Four out of five doctors recommend another doctor.
- Join the army, see the world, meet interesting people, and kill them.
- Never share a foxhole with anyone braver than yourself.
- Don't forget your weapon was made by the lowest bidder.
- The older I get, the better I used to be.
- Proofread carefully to see if you any words out.
- Never wave to your friends at an auction. (William Broadersen)
- There are 3 kinds of people: those who can count and those who can't.
- I don't have a solution, but I admire the problem.
- If everyone else gets a flu shot, you don't need one. (Richard Stump)
- You don't have to be in *Who's Who* to know what's what. (Bennett Cerf)

Another one-liner quotation format is the *probing question* that looks at the absurdity of what we say and do. It sometimes poses unanswerable, nonsensical, and even very logical, but funny questions. They can also be labeled "semi-deep thoughts," although I haven't been able to detect the content difference between a "probing question" and a "semi-deep thought." The distinction is too deep for me to grasp. Consistent with all of the preceding types of quotations, these questions do not have to be read to your audience. They can be unmasked on a chalkboard, overhead, or slide. Here are a few examples adapted from Malloy (1996), Mayer (1996), O'Brien (1995), and Whaley (1992):

- What do we say to God when he sneezes?
- Did Adam and Eve have belly-buttons?
- How many Americans are currently frozen in the hope of one day coming back to life?
- What percentage of nuts do squirrels lose because they forget where they put them?
- Why do squirrels keep trying to cross the road after seeing what happened to their buddies when they tried?
- Where does the fat go when someone loses 30 lbs?
- In what type of container is Styrofoam shipped?
- Who hears the Pope's confession?
- Did bald eagles ever have hair?
- Why did Kamikaze pilots wear helmets?
- Is there a split between mind and body, and, if so, which is better to have?

- If 7-11 is open 24 hours a day, 365 days a year, why are there locks on the doors?
- If a cow laughed really hard, would milk come out her nose?
- Why isn't "phonetic" spelled the way it sounds?
- Why isn't "palindrome" spelled the same way backwards?
- Why doesn't "onomatopoeia" sound like what it is?
- What is another word for "thesaurus"?
- Why is "abbreviation" such a long word?
- Why do "fat chance" and "slim chance" mean the same thing?
- Why do "flammable" and "inflammable" mean the same thing?
- Why does your nose "run" and your feet "smell"?
- How can someone "draw a blank"?
- How can someone actually be "beside oneself"?
- Why isn't there such a thing as a "rhetorical" answer?
- Why do we drive on parkways and park on driveways?
- Why is it that when you transport something by car, it's called a "shipment," but when you transport something by ship, it's called "cargo"?
- If pro is the opposite of con, is progress the opposite of congress?
- Why is it, whether you sit up or sit down, the result is the same?
- Why isn't a "building" called a "built"?
- Why are "apartments" all stuck together?
- Whose cruel idea was it to put an "s" in the word "lisp"?
- Why is it that when you're driving and looking for an address, you turn down the radio or tell everybody to be quiet?
- If 75% of all accidents happen within 5 miles of home, why not move 10 miles away?
- If olive oil comes from olives, from what does baby oil come?
- Why are there Braille dots on the keypad of the drive-up ATM?
- Is it illegal to run into a crowded fire and yell "Theater!"?
- Isn't a question mark really an exclamation point with osteoporosis?
- Does the French military use Dijon mustard gas?
- When termites finish dining on toothpicks, do they clean their teeth with pieces of spinach?
- When amphibians finish eating, do they have to wait 1 hour before getting out of the water?
- Do poker playing dogs own paintings of humans playing fetch?

An extension of the one-liner quotation format is the *multi-liner quotation*. One or more lines are used to build more tension for the punch line at the end than the single quotation. Further, it has the added advantage of familiarity similar to the twisted expression format. The lines of the quotation are well-known sayings or quotes. They provide the expected element before the unexpected twist is introduced. Three examples are given below:

Lead-in: "Here is the latest version of a popular expression which is more meaningful to me at this stage of life":

Multi-liner 1: Been There,
Done That,
CAN'T REMEMBER!

or

Lead-in: "Sometimes you need to be careful about what you put in print, especially if it's published, compared to what you say. It can come back to haunt you or worse. For example,"

Multi-liner 2: GOD IS DEAD.
Nietzsche (1886)

NIETZSCHE IS DEAD.
GOD (1900)

or

Lead-in: "Let's begin with a few basic truths":

Multi-liner 3: GOD Is Love.
Love Is Blind.
Stevie Wonder Is Blind.
∴ Stevie Wonder Is GOD.

Any of these quotations can be presented orally, visually, or a combination of both. The latter two options seem to have the strongest impact. One effective low-risk method for presenting multi-liner 1 and 2 is to prepare the entire quote on one transparency with big, bold lettering, use a cover sheet over the transparency, and then reveal each line or one quotation with the author at a time as the audience reads. Nothing has to be said. For multi-liner 3, the build-up of tension is slower as you uncover each line. After the third line is shown, say "therefore," to bring the tension to a peak before you reveal the punch line. Timing is crucial with this format in order to allow the audience to build their anticipation for the punch.

Cartoons. Cartoons are one of the oldest and most widely used formats for political satire and social commentary on practices and values. They are presented in virtually every print and electronic media form currently available. In fact, you're probably not going to believe this (but I'm going to tell you anyway), there is a statistics textbook that consists totally of cartoons (Gonick & Smith, 1993). Given the 1000s of cartoons we encounter everywhere, how can they be used as an instructional tool? At this point, it is reasonable to assume that there is really no need to create your own cartoons, and few of us even possess the combination of artistic and humor gifts to do that. The task, then, is to select cartoons that are both funny and apropos to your message.

Cartoons can be injected anywhere in a lecture or presentation. I have seen some presenters use cartoons throughout their entire speech. It is best to link your selected jocular cartoons to the content of your message. The cartoons may be in a single panel or multiple panel format.

The visual presentation of cartoons is crucial to their success. An overhead or slide must display a large image of the cartoon characters and any verbal material. The single panel cartoon should be easy to see and interpret at a glance from anywhere in the room. Avoid complicated graphics with a lot of detail that may require too much time to read or even a second reading. Depending on the structure of the cartoon, you may want to pause for a few seconds for the audience to process the cartoon and then read the caption if it is a strong punch line. Your verbal delivery plus the visual element may produce a stronger response than the visual alone. Experiment with both methods for different cartoons. For cartoons with multiple panels, reveal only one panel at a time with the punch line, if there is one. Each panel builds its own tension as you move toward the final panel and punch. One popular cartoon on the notion of compulsiveness is shown below:

Callahan, J. (1990). *Do not disturb any further.*
New York: William Morrow.

Multiple-Choice Items. This has become one of the most popular humor formats in humor books and on television because everyone has taken multiple-choice tests and can relate easily to the format. There is even a book that is a clever parody of the traditional Scholastic Aptitude Test (S.A.T.) in multiple-choice format (Davis, 1991). The issue is how to maximize its laughter potential in a presentation. As indicated in the previous chapter, the stem or question is the serious element that builds the tension for the choices which are the punch lines. It is the three to five choices that reduce your risk of bombing compared to a stand-up joke or one-liner which has only one punch line. The multiple-choice format and the top 10 list format to follow essentially employ a shotgun approach to punch lines. Instead of only one punch line, the multiple-choice item may have five and, obviously, the top 10 list has (Duuuuhhh!) 19. It is not expected that all choices will be winners. In fact, if only one choice, particularly the last one, succeeds, you've got a winner because the other choices contribute to the tension building element in the humor. Only preliminary tryouts with friendly faculty, secretaries, or students may reveal the best choice to place last. Once the item is presented in your classes or to a large audience of your peers, the winning choice(s) can change. Personal experience suggests that the responses to the choices will vary among undergraduate and graduate students and the courses you teach.

The wording of the stem and choices must be chosen with great care. First, the stem should be short and crisp to create a humorous situation and build-up of tension so that the audience's interest is peaked before the choices are presented. Second, prepare the choices as one-liners. Each one should pack a punch and be so polished that it will jump off the screen into the minds of the audience and create a funny picture. Only trial-and-error will indicate which choices work and which ones need revision or replacement. As you obtain audience feedback, order the choices in terms of progressive funniness. This will help build tension as each succeeding choice is revealed leading to the super-punch. The number of choices will vary according to how each choice contributes. There should be no dead choices. Each should elicit one of the 15 stages of laughter (see Chapter 1). In other words, each one should be humorous enough to produce a smile, a smirk, or maybe a chortle. You cannot expect convulsive laughter after each choice. Based on your experience, select between three and five of the funniest choices you can write. An alternative strategy is to structure the item first as a top 10 list, and then choose the winners from among the 10 choices.

Although several multiple-choice items were presented in the previous chapter to illustrate the "build-up of tension," here are a few more with slightly different formats, numbers of choices, and generic and professional content:

Generic Content Items

- Which one of the following expressions is an OXYMORON?

  A. Amtrak schedule

  B. express mail

  C. newspaper facts

  D. athletic scholarship

  E. legal brief

or

- A "SCUB" is a (an)

  A. insect with 1000 eyes, 500 for distance and 500 for reading.

  B. creature with the body of a squid and the head of an IRS agent.

  C. single's game played with a roulette wheel and a bottle of Kaopectate.

  D. wild animal with the head of a giraffe and the body of a giraffe, though not the same giraffe.

or

- According to former Surgeon General C. Everett Koop, patients should AVOID physicians whose:

  A. favorite hobby is taxidermy.

  B. waiting room wall has a sailfish on it that's still alive.

  C. diplomas are autographed by Dr. Kevorkian.

  D. favorite movie is *The Silence of the Lambs.*

or

- Which one of the following "real" classified ads in the *Baltimore Sun* received the largest response? (Adapted from Mayer, 1996, pp. 37–40)

  A. Used Cars: Why go elsewhere to be cheated? Come here first.

  B. Dinner Special: Turkey $2.35
     Chicken or Beef $2.25
     Children $2.00

  C. Auto Repair Service. Free pick-up and delivery. Try us once, you'll never go anywhere again.

  D. Mixing bowl set designed to please a cook with round bottom for efficient beating.

  E. Man wanted to work in dynamite factory. Must be willing to travel.

Professional Content Items

- Which one of the following actions is ILL-ADVISED during your thesis defense?

  A. At the beginning, say: "Will you all please rise and sing *God Save the Queen?*"

  B. Hang a piñata resembling your thesis chairperson in the middle of the room and smack it with a baseball bat when you're provoked.

  C. After the first round of questioning, stop for a moment to lead your Committee in the WAVE!

  D. When the questioning is over, say: "As I light this candle, please hold hands, bow your heads, and meditate on the word PASS!"

  E. If the Committee announces that you passed, spike your thesis, high five each Committee member, and do the "Macarena."

or

- Which one of the following is a "MURPHY'S LAW" version of your annual meeting experience?

  A. The most boring presentation always goes overtime.

  B. The BEST session of the day is opposite the session in which YOU are a participant.

  C. The paper you want most at a session is the only one not available.

  D. At a publisher's booth in the Exhibit Hall, the single copy of a textbook you urgently need to review for your course has already been reserved by someone else for pick-up on Friday.

  E. The five receptions to which you were invited are on the SAME night from 6–9 P.M. at DIFFERENT hotels.

or

- What is the key ingredient in the NEW "Quadruple Blind Experimental Design" intended to eliminate all major sources of human bias?

  A. Participants don't know what they're getting.

  B. Treatment administrators don't know what they're giving.

  C. Research assistants don't know what they're gathering.

  D. Researchers don't know what they're doing.

The success of the multiple-choice format is contingent not only on how it is structured and the funniness of the content, but also on how it is presented. There are three options: (1) simply read it, (2) visually display it on an overhead transparency or slide, or (3) a combination of (1) and (2). Studies have indicated that the verbal-visual combo seems to be the best strategy to produce the strongest impact. (See Chapter 5 for further evidence.)

Extending the same techniques described previously for quotations, prepare the complete item on one colored overhead transparency in big bold print so it can be seen and read easily by the audience. We know different colors evoke different emotions: *red* represents fire, passion, or blushing, *yellow* is warm or jaundice, *blue* is cool or dead (as in Code Blue), *green* is sickly or moldy (as in my lunch), *pink* is putrid, and *purple* is just plain nasty. Humorous material presented with colored letters and/or on a colored background can contribute to the emotional effect.

Both the visual presentation of the item and your "dramatic" verbal delivery are required to tweak out its maximum laughter potential. (Also see Chapter 5 for additional tips on delivery.) The following steps are recommended:

1. Place the transparency on the overhead with a blank sheet of paper over or under it.
   a. This is your transparency.
   b. This is your transparency on paper.
   c. Any questions?
2. When you and the audience are ready, move the sheet down to reveal only the stem and read it (a.k.a. "revelation" method).
3. Pause for a couple of moments to build the tension and anticipation in the audience before presenting the choices.
4. Move the sheet down to reveal choice A and read it. (If there is immediate laughter, wait until it stops; otherwise, keep moving. DO NOT wait for the laughter.)
5. Repeat for choices B, C, etc.
6. For the final choice, introduce it with "or choice E" or "and finally," pause, then read it. (Remember this should be your super-punch choice.)

Top 10 Lists. Popularized by David Letterman over the past decade, the top 10 list has become a widely used technique in public speaking everywhere. It can be employed as an opening joke, a method for summarizing content during a presentation, and as a closing humorous or even nonhumorous summary. It's neat, clean, gets to the points quickly, and can succeed as a low-risk strategy even when most of the choices don't receive laughter. (It certainly helps to have a band cue the audience at the beginning, before the number 1 choice, and after the number 1 choice, although Paul Shaffer's band probably would not be available.)

If we talk about a shotgun approach to humor, the 10 choices which are the buckshot should be written with the same meticulous care given to the multiple-choice item choices. As a variation of the multiple-choice format, it is much more difficult to write. Developing four or five funny punch lines is usually tough enough. (Maybe that's why Letterman pays a dozen writers.) Certain types of material lend themselves to list format better than others, and Letterman's four books (Letterman et al., 1990, 1991, 1995, 1996) and the availability of top 10s on the Internet provide useful starting points from which to generate ideas.

The structure, content, and delivery of a top 10 list are a direct extension of everything recommended for the multiple-choice format. The introduction and ending are slightly different because it is a list, not a test item. Further, you can use Letterman's execution or put your own spin on the list. Personalizing Letterman's approach would involve the following:

1. A lead-in read to the audience such as: "Here in my left hand is this (morning's, afternoon's or evenings') top 10 list. From my home office in (your city, state), here are the..."
2. Reveal heading of the top 10 list on the transparency as you read it.
3. Pause just as with the stem in multiple-choice format to build tension in the audience.
4. Reveal number 10 punch line only on the transparency and read it.
5. Repeat for numbers 9 through 2.
6. Say, "And the number 1 (repeat heading of list) is."
7 Pause to build tension.
8. Reveal number 1 punch line and read it.

Here are a few top 10 lists as additional examples to the two lists presented in Chapter 2:

Top 10 Newsworthy Events Happening This Week
(One-liners adapted from Kipfer and Strnad, 1996)

10. Due to numerous oil spills, Bumble Bee has announced that tuna will now be available in unleaded regular, plus, and premium.
 9. Following the lifting of the 55 MPH speed limit, Congress has now approved the yellow traffic light to officially mean "floor it."

8. Faster acting laxatives have now made it possible for runners to break the 3 minute mile.

7. Several UFOs recently landed in the Midwest and they are actually fuzzy, which explains all of those blurry photographs.

6. Due to deflation of the English language, a picture is now worth only 750 words.

5. TV/VCR controls are now being built into furniture so couch potatoes won't have to waste energy reaching for the remote.

4. Bill Gates just bought the earth and renamed it "Windows on the World."

3. Scientists have found that the major downside of cryogenics is nasty freezer burn.

2. Mattel has introduced the new Divorced Barbie, which comes with all of Ken's possessions.

1. The name of the proposed national health insurance program is DON'T GET SICK!

Top 10 Bumper Stickers

10. I Owe, I Owe, It's Off to Work I Go.

9. If Money Could Talk, It Would Say: Bye Bye!"

8. It's Lonely at the Top, But You Eat Better.

7. My Karma Ran Over Your Dogma.

6. I Brake for Brick Walls.

5. Friends Don't Let Friends Drive Naked.

4. I May Be Fat, But You're Ugly, and I Can Lose Weight.

3. My Worst Day Fishing Is Better Than My Best Day Working.

2. I Don't Care Who's On Board, What You're Driving, or Where You'd Rather Be.

1. All Men Are Idiots, and I Married the King!

Top 10 Automobile Accident Descriptions from the Secret Files of Insurance Agents
(One-liners adapted from Mayer, 1996, pp. 43–46)

10. A truck backed through my windshield into my wife's face.

9. The guy was all over the road. I had to swerve a number of times before I hit him.

8. In my attempt to kill a fly, I drove into a telephone pole.

7. The accident was caused by me waving to the man I hit last week.

6. I had been driving my car for 40 years when I fell asleep at the wheel and had an accident.

5. To avoid hitting the bumper of the car in front, I struck the pedestrian.

4. The telephone pole was approaching fast. I was attempting to swerve out of its path when it struck my front end!

3. I saw the slow-moving, sad-faced old man as he bounced off the hood of my car.

2. The trees were passing me in an orderly row at 50 MPH when suddenly one of them stepped out into my path.

1. The pedestrian had no idea which direction to go, so I ran over him.

Berk's Top 10 Diet Tips

10. If no one sees you eat it, it has no calories.

9. If you drink a diet soda with a candy bar, they cancel each other out.

8. When eating with someone else, calories don't count if you both eat the same thing.

7. The calories from candy or donuts consumed while driving are burned up at the rate of one item per mile.

6. If you snack while cooking, the calories disappear because you're doing something nice for your family.

5. Food used for medical purposes NEVER counts, e.g., hot chocolate with marshmallows, banana splits, and Sara Lee cheesecake.

4. Anything eaten after midnight or after you've gone to bed counts toward the next day's calories, but it doesn't matter because you won't remember it anyway.

3. If you fatten up everyone else around you, then you look thinner.

2. Movie-related foods don't count because they are simply part of the entire entertainment experience and not a part of one's personal fuel, e.g., Milk Duds, popcorn with butter, and chocolate covered peanuts/raisins.

1. Eating while standing up with your fingers is half the calories as eating sitting down using a fork or spoon.

Anecdotes. Stories or descriptions of personal experiences that are true, with maybe a little exaggeration, are excellent icebreakers to warm-up an audience. The challenge is to identify funny stories or those that can be presented so that they have a humorous impact. Not all anecdotes are designed intentionally with punch lines at the end as prepared jokes are. That is why they are considered low-risk humor. The success of telling your story does not hinge only on the impact of a punch line. The humor may emerge in your delivery, that is, your dramatization of the experience. The audience may or may not laugh at the "right" places. That's okay. If there is a punch line, then the build-up of tension in the delivery of the story is critical. Here is a true story I have used at the beginning of several presentations:

Fear of Speaking

As I begin this presentation, I have to admit to you that at one key point in my career I had developed a fear of speaking in front of audiences such as yourself. I know some of you may not believe this, but my fear was the result of a specific incident in graduate school. In one of my doctoral courses, I was required to make a presentation in front of the class.

Let me set the stage for you. I walked up to the front of the class and stood between the chalkboard on the wall behind me and a six-foot long table which was in front of me. There was a depth of about three feet between the chalkboard and the table. The tile floor in the room had just been freshly waxed. You could tell from the shine. The day before our hero had new leather soles and heels put on his shoes.

I began my presentation. At one point I remember talking while writing something on the chalkboard. As I stepped to turn to the front, my right foot skidded forward and I went splat on the floor on my back under the table. There I lay, prostrate under the table. What do you do? First, it hits you that there is no ceremonious way to get up. Basically, I had two options: either get up facing the class and continue the presentation or take the chicken's way out and get up facing the board and continue. I picked the chicken's way out. I got up and continued writing on the board as though nothing had happened. I was afraid to turn around because the students were probably laughing inside or look like they were going to burst out with laughter.

The best part of this whole episode occurred after the class. One of the students came up to me and asked, "Ron, during your presentation you disappeared for a while. (Oh, you noticed?) Where did you go?" Oh, I slipped out to run a couple of errands!

This experience had to be one of life's most embarrassing moments. This was before the show, *Funniest Home Videos*. You may have noticed before I began here that I was looking down at the floor to check my footing and to evaluate the carpeting or astroturf. Of course, you noticed I'm wearing cleats. (Just kidding!)

A few other stories with specific themes that I've used, but are not mine, are given below:

It's a Matter of Perspective

A Texas farmer was visiting a farmer in Georgia to learn about some new agricultural methods. The Texas farmer was chatting with the Georgia farmer and said, "By the way, how big is your farm?" The Georgia farmer answered, "It's about 2 miles straight down that way, and then about a mile across along the stream, and then another couple of miles over the hills way over yonder."

The Texan thought, "That's pretty big." The Georgia farmer then turned to the Texas farmer and asked, "How big is your farm?"

"Well, back in Texas, I can get into my pick-up truck at sunrise and drive straight ahead on my property and keep on driving and at sunset, I will still be driving on my farm."

The Georgia farmer shook his head and said, (Pause) "Yeah, I used to have a pick-up truck like that too!" (Adapted from Wright and Wright, 1985, p. 56)

Survival

Two hikers were walking through the woods when they suddenly confronted a giant bear. Immediately, one of the men took off his boots, pulled out a pair of track shoes, and began putting them on. "What are you doing?" his companion cried. "We can't outrun that bear, even with jogging shoes."

"Who cares about the bear?" the first hiker replied. "All I have to worry about (pause) is outrunning you." (Adapted from Wright and Wright, 1985, p. 57)

Standards of Quality

I was on the road and having trouble with my car, so I pulled into a service station just off the highway. I was a little leery about going to a place I didn't know, so I watched one of the mechanics work for a while. He was amazing. He changed the oil without spilling a drop. He wiped his hands before touching the upholstery, and he pulled the car out of the garage very slowly and carefully. I was so impressed that I said to the guy pumping gas, "Boy, your mechanic really does a good job, doesn't he?" He said, "Why not? (pause) It's his car." (Iapoce, 1988, p. 191)

Skits/Dramatizations. One creative method to begin any presentation is the skit. Using music and a few simple props or a costume can be a great warm-up and tone setter. The trick is to think of a television, stage, or movie character with whom most everyone can relate and develop a short skit that can be the springboard for your presentation. There are a couple of winners I have used in my classes, which have ranged in size from 5 to 100 students. The skits also have been executed in conference presentations with audiences of 250 to 1500.

A. Home Improvement: The first skit is a take-off on the popular sitcom, *Home Improvement.* It uses the metaphor of tools which can be linked to the content of numerous topics, such as the tools of any job or profession (e.g., teaching) as well as specific statistical, measurement, or research tools.

> **WARNING:** You should not attempt to use this metaphor at home. You must be a trained professional like me. It should only be applied to on-the-job performances, such as class lectures, research presentations, and court appearances.

Here are the steps I follow:

1. Prepare props in advance (chair, bag with toolbelt, tape player, transparencies)

   a. Chair — Before the presentation, place a chair next to the overhead projector or lectern.

   b. Bag — Use a backpack or some other bag to conceal the belt and tools. Set the bag on the chair seat so it is easily accessible. The element of surprise in the transformation from suit and tie (regardless of gender) to the toolbelt is significant to the success of the skit.

c. Player — A small tape player (about 5" x 7"), powered by four AA batteries, is adequate for a room size up to 100 students. For large lecture halls, theater-style rooms, or auditoriums, place the player near the lectern microphone or lay a lavaliere microphone over the speaker. Make sure the tape is set in the player correctly and the volume is at an appropriate level. Test it before the presentation; then rewind the tape (one time I forgot!).

d. Transparencies — Prepare two transparencies, in color if possible. The first specifies the topic for "Tool Time," such as Teaching, Statistical, Performance Assessment, and Research. For example,

RESEARCH

"TOOL TIME"

The second transparency identifies you as the "Tool Man" or "Tool Woman," as follows:

RON

"THE TOOL MAN"

BERK

Place the first transparency on the overhead with a cover sheet.

2. Say, "I think we're ready to begin."

3. Press play button on player to begin theme music from *Home Improvement.*

4. As the music begins,

a. Take off your jacket

b. Hang it around the back of the chair

c. Pull toolbelt out of the bag

d. Put on the belt

e. Place heavier tools (kept at the bottom of bag), such as a hammer and drill, into their compartments or holsters.

f. (*Optional:* Put on suspenders; I use bright yellow tape-measure design suspenders to keep the belt from falling to the floor with 300 lbs. of tools.)

It usually takes all of the theme music to get the belt on, tools in position, and suspenders unraveled (I almost strangled myself once), even with lots of practice. The dye has been cast. You better do something clever next.

5. Stop the tape and readjust lectern microphone or reattach the lavaliere microphone to your suspenders, if necessary.

6. Remove cover sheet from the overhead, turn on projector, and then move into an aisle close to your students or audience.

7. Say, "What time is it?" The students will respond unevenly with "Tool Time" because they're not sure what to do. Say, "That was pathetic; I'm going to give you another chance. This time I want the *(Dean, everyone in this building, etc.)* to hear what time it is. Are you ready? Okay, what time is it?" The response this time is thunderous. Your students have been transformed from spectators to participants.

8. Put second transparency on the projector and say, "I'm Ron, The Tool Man, Berk, and I'd like to welcome you to this special edition of Tool Time. This *(morning, afternoon, evening)* I am going to be talking about tools, the tools of research. Some are the old traditional, reliable tools, such as screwdrivers and hammers (hold them up in both hands); others are new, cutting edge, high tech tools. However, sometimes for the job we have to perform, we may need more POWER! (pause) In that case, may I suggest (pull power drill out of belt and hold up) the new Binford turbo-charged 50,000 RPM research plugger. This baby will fill in any holes in your research design in a jiff. It is so effective, no one will detect any sources of invalidity, not even those stodgy reviewers of the research proposals we send to Washington."

9. Lead into the content of your presentation.

(Note: Since I always teach or present alone, I haven't found a way to work the character of Al "The Flannel" Borland into the skit.)

B. *Mister Rogers' Neighborhood:* The second skit I have found useful in a variety of applications is a take-off on *Mister Rogers' Neighborhood.* This one is much simpler than the previous one, but still has a positive impact. I have presented a lot of topics under the heading "Mister Researcher's Neighborhood" and "Mister Rono's Neighborhood." You could probably think of other variations of that theme. Here are the steps:

1. Prepare props in advance (chair, clothes, tape player, transparency)

   a. Chair — Before the presentation, place a chair in front of the room so it is visible to everyone.

   b. Clothes — Hide a pair of tennis shoes under the chair and place a cardigan or zippered sweater rolled up in a ball on the seat. Cover both with paper or plastic bags. No one usually anticipates what those props mean even when they see them.

c. Player — Prepare the tape player as in *Home Improvement* skit (see step 1c).

d. Transparency — Prepare one transparency, in color if possible, with the following, for example,

MISTER RESEARCHER'S

NEIGHBORHOOD

Place this transparency on the overhead with a cover sheet.

2. Say, "I think we're ready to begin."

3. Press play button on player to begin theme music and remove cover sheet on the projector.

4. As the music begins,

   a. Take off your jacket

   b. Hang it around the back of the chair

   c. Put on the sweater while standing

   d. Sit down in the chair and remove one shoe. Reach under the chair and put on first tennis shoe. Repeat for all of your other feet.

5. Walk back to the player and stop the tape. Readjust lectern microphone or reattach the lavaliere microphone to your sweater, if necessary.

6. Say, "Welcome to Mister Researcher's Neighborhood. I'm Mister Researcher. This *(morning, afternoon, evening)* I'd like to talk to you about *(topic)*."

7. Lead into the content of your presentation.

Even though this skit is a lower key beginning than "Tool Time," it can be very effective in its own way, plus it can be an introduction to virtually any topic.

What makes these skits so successful is that they possess the three essential elements of humor defined previously. The music is also a key ingredient because it appeals directly to the students' emotions and conjures up funny images of "Tim" and "Fred."

C. Other Skits: Consider the possibilities of other skits built around theme music from Star Trek (see Chapter 6), *Jeopardy!* (see Chapter 6), *Masterpiece Theatre, Rocky, Chariots of Fire,* and *The Odd Couple* (for two presenters). I have developed routines for these themes related to specific content in my classes. You have to experiment and let your imagination fly. Remember this is "low-risk" humor that requires practice to execute, but there is no punch line. These skits can certainly put the "fun" back into your teaching or presentations if you need a humor stimulant.

Ad-libs that Aren't. Previously the "ad-lib" was discussed as a type of high-risk humor in response to a person's question or comment. There's another type that would be considered low risk: responses to interruptions or distractions during a presentation that are either your fault or an equipment failure. As professors, these unusual "events" seem to occur with some regularity in our classes. For example, how many times have you experienced the following?

a. Lost your thought or place while talking?

b. Garbled or slurred a sentence (or punch line)?

c. Microphone goes dead?

d. Received a blast of microphone feedback?

e. Lights flicker or go out?

f. Loud crashing or other noises (e.g., fire-engine sirens)?

g. Projector light burns out?

h. Room is too cold?

I. Room is too hot?

Every one of these distractions represents an opportunity for humor. A timely spontaneous response that is humorous is the best way to put your students or audience at ease and regain their attention. After all, if you can't stay focused and get back on track, what are they supposed to do? Take advantage of the opportunities as they arise in your classes to try out ad-libs. This will prepare you if the situation occurs during a presentation to a large audience at a conference. The audience will admire your ability to ad-lib. Little do they know. . . Here are several suggested ad-libs, some of which were recommended by Iapoce (1988):

- Well, this seems to be going well. (Anything that goes wrong)

- Sometimes we can say the most with silence. However, not this time, but sometimes. (During a pause where you lost your thought)

- If anyone wants to jump right in, please feel free. (During a pause where you lost your place)

- It sounds like her interview for the new assistant professor position didn't go very well. (Baby crying outside of classroom)

- Sorry, I rented these lips (or it's my first day with my new mouth). (Garble words)

- Later, I'll pass out a translation of that sentence. (Garble words)

- Evidently someone has heard this lecture (or presentation) before. (Microphone goes dead)

- Oh, by the way, how many of you can read lips? (Microphone goes dead)

- Let this be a lesson, what can happen when you buy your sound system from K- Mart. (Microphone goes dead or feedback)
- This concludes the musical portion of my presentation. (Microphone feedback or loud noises)
- This was only a test. If this had been an actual emergency ... (Microphone feedback or other weird noises)
- Where is Edison when you need him? (Lights in room or projector light goes out)
- I told the Dean to pay the gas and electric bill. (Lights flicker or go out)
- I knew I should have used the low-tech chalkboard. (Projector light goes out)
- Was it something I said, God? (Lights flicker or go out)
- Why do I have the feeling I'll be alone when the lights come back on? (Lights go out)
- I have to admit to you that you are all participants in a study of cryogenics. (Room too cold)
- Does anyone else have frost on your glasses? (Room too cold)
- I tried to turn up (or lower) the thermostat. But it was already frozen (or melted). (Room too cold or too hot)

> **WARNING:** Here we go again. Another serious section. Believe me I'm not trying to gag you with boredom, just set forth some rules for the types of humor that are appropriate and inappropriate. If I didn't, I could be cited for NCAA violations and suspended for a year without play.

Offensive Humor

This type of humor was mentioned at the beginning of this chapter as a risk of spontaneous humor. However, the consequences of using offensive humor in preparing "low-risk" humorous material or any other form of humor used in the classroom or professional presentation are so serious that it requires special attention in this section.

Some faculty have asked, "What's wrong with using offensive humor (or blue material)?" The answer boils down to the difference between our roles as teachers and presenters versus the professional comedian's role as entertainer. Table 1 lists the major differences beginning with the purpose of the humor. We are using it as an instructional or teaching tool to improve the effectiveness of communicating our substantive message. The attitude of some professional comedians is "I don't care who I offend." Anyone or anything is fair game for their humor. Another difference in these uses of humor is the options available in response to an offensive joke. If we're offended in a nightclub, we can walk out; if the television program or movie is offensive, we can turn it off. Our students or members of our audience do not have those options; they can't walk out (actually they can) because they'll miss the content presented and they certainly can't turn us off. What they can do is tune us out, grit their teeth, or harbor anger or resentment toward us. We've just misused the tool of humor. Can you think of one advantage for using offensive humor that can offset any of the preceding disadvantages?

Humorous material that is developed in advance can be tested and edited to usually prevent any offensive content. Ask colleagues, secretaries, family members, or friends whether they perceive anything that could be offensive to anyone. We have to be extremely careful as to what is acceptable in-bounds humor and what is unacceptable out-of-bounds humor (Bryant et al., 1980a).

Inappropriate Targets. Here is a list of seven categories or targets of offensive humor that I try to avoid at all times: (1) put-downs of any individual, including a popular, entertainment, or political personality; (2) put-downs of any group based on ethnicity, race, gender, religion, or sexual orientation; (3) sarcasm and ridicule; (4) sexual content and innuendo; (5) profanity and vulgarity; (6) humor about physical disabilities and characteristics (e.g., fat, short, blond, pregnant) and mental handicaps; and (7) humor about extremely sensitive issues (e.g., AIDS, abortion, divorce, personal tragedies).

A rather cursory review of these categories should suggest that the heart of Leno's and Letterman's monologues and most sitcoms is offensive jokes. The reasons people like or dislike those comedians or particular sitcoms may be related to what offends them.

Appropriate Targets. If the preceding categories and targets of humor are off limits, then what targets are acceptable? Rather than putting down a colleague or anyone well-respected by your audience, uplift or boost them with positive humor. It has been said the "the richest laugh is at no one's expense." Choose the targets of your humor very carefully. There is one simple, ironclad rule to follow when selecting the "butt" of a joke: Make sure you choose a big enough target or "butt" (Iapoce, 1988). This is known as the "Big Butt" Theory of humor. (I just made that up.) For example, the president of the university or association, the institution itself, or practices of our profession may be immune to certain types of humor. However, it should still not be malicious or denigrate any person or his or her position. Humor that focuses on characteristics or practices that are obviously not true, outrageously exaggerated, or relatively unimportant can be very successful.

Table 1
What's Wrong With Using Offensive Humor?

Factor	Humor as a Teaching Strategy	Professional Comedians/ Movies/Sitcoms
Purpose of humor	• To facilitate learning by better connecting with students or audience • To reduce anxiety • To improve attitudes toward subject	• To entertain
Excuses for using offensive humor (blue material)	• Students and faculty talk that way outside of class • Students and faculty tell "blue" jokes all the time	• That's what people want to hear (not true) • That's the way people talk (set yourself apart from everyone else) • Every comedian's doing it (not true, but be different, original, unique)
Reasons for not using offensive humor	• Inappropriate in the classroom and professional presentations • Unnecessary, if you're creative • Can produce the opposite of the intended effect (humor backfires)	• Reduces size of your potential audience • Limits your marketability (makes less money) • Limits your creativity • Stunts your comedic growth
Response options to offensive humor	• You set a bad example (role model) for your students • Students have nowhere to go; must return to class • Can't turn you off; instead tune you out • Cringe, withdraw, tighten-up, or become angry or resentful	• Leave the night club or movie • Turn off the TV • Do not have to watch the comedian or program ever again

Self-Effacing Humor

Probably one of the most convenient, safe, and nonoffensive targets for humor is YOU. The late humor columnist, Erma Bombeck, acknowledged the value of this type of humor early in her career, "Long ago it became apparent there were only two people in the world I could take a crack at in print without being sued or severely criticized: Adolf Hitler and me!" Making mock of yourself, your professional accomplishments, and experiences furnish a wealth of material for the humor, plus it is extremely effective. Given your lofty position as academician (granted, some of you are loftier than others), such humor gives the audience the impression that you are human, real, approachable, in other words, one of them. You should never set yourself up as being superior to your audience. Being modest or humble about what you have attained and using "self-downs" as the humor mechanism to communicate that demeanor will win more points with any audience than the impression of being arrogant or pretentious.

Self-effacing or self-deprecating humor in the form of "self-downs" reveals your faults and weaknesses. This gives your audience a feeling of comfort to see their faults reflected in a person of power like their professor or speaker. This type of humor doesn't diminish their respect for you; in fact, it increases their respect, because you project a sense of confidence and security by being able to poke fun at yourself. A few comedians, such as Woody Allen and Rodney Dangerfield, have built their routines around the concept of being a loser, which takes the technique of self-effacing humor to the extreme. Dangerfield's "I don't get no respect" character has been very successful at getting the respect of just about everybody because, as the late Jack Benny remarked, "no one gets respect."

When in doubt about the target of your humor, use yourself. Moreover, systematically substitute yourself as the target in much of your humor and you will become more believable and appreciated.

Writing Your Own Humorous Material

Based on all of the forms of humor and examples presented in this chapter, how do you begin to write your own material? Here are six steps:

1. *Pick a format:* Select one of the formats that strikes you as appropriate to your style and application. Suppose it's top 10 lists.

2. *Analyze examples:* Locate examples, such as those in this book or others that have been published (see Letterman's four books listed in Chapter 4), to serve as prototypes for both form and substance. Analyze what makes those examples funny to you. Would your students or colleagues respond the same way?

3. *Select one example:* Choose one example that seems to have potential. Remember it was probably written by a large team of highly overpaid comedy writers!

4. *Build your own format:* If the example is workable and maybe one or two of the 10 one-liners strikes you as hilarious, write a few of your own to construct a four- or five-choice multiple-choice item at first. If you can dream up five more choices, you'll have your top 10 list.

5. *Evaluate your one-liners:* Determine the quality and effectiveness of your choices in terms of structure, content, and impact. Your answers to the following seven questions can guide this assessment and pinpoint parts of your list that probably need revision:

   • Does it satisfy the criterion of incongruity?
   • Would the content be understood by your audience?
   • Is there a build-up of tension?
   • Is the unexpected twist strong enough (i.e., absurd, exaggerated, bizarre) to be funny?
   • Is it too long (wordy) or too short (not enough information or build-up)?
   • Does it present a visual (or graphic) image that is hilarious?
   • Could it be interpreted as offensive to anyone?

6. *Revise your one-liners:* Based on your evaluation, modify your material as many times as you need until you feel it's ready to be tested.

Writing humorous material takes practice, lots of it. After all, it's a profession by itself. An excellent resource for writing and revising one-liners with 86 practice exercises ("workouts") plus loads of examples is Perret's workbook (1990).

Field Testing Your Material

Once you have a few one-liners, a multiple-choice item, top 10 list, or anecdote that meets the preceding criteria, test it for immediate impact on your secretary, a few colleagues, previous students, or friends and family members if the content is appropriate. Since most of us are probably novices in this area of comedy writing, it would be very encouraging to receive positive responses from our testees (this term has always made me uncomfortable). Reinforcement is reeeally important. Therefore, I suggest that you choose your testees carefully.

If you know office mates who will usually laugh at almost anything, I'd recommend starting with them. There are usually a few jolly folks in every department. I have three dear colleagues in my department who are always my first choices for testing new material. If they don't find the stuff funny, no one will. Based on our friendship, I also do not hesitate to ask them a couple of the questions in the preceding section about which I have some doubts, such as whether all of my students would understand it based on their age or gender and whether it is offensive. Their feedback is extremely valuable. Your colleagues may notice flaws you never caught. The testees' reaction to the funniness of your material as well as its appropriateness will usually indicate the directions for your revision.

After this preliminary field test has been completed with your favorite laughers, it's time to move to the next level. At this point, conceptualize a graduated scale of laughers—from those who will usually laugh at anything (level 1 testees) to those who are more "discriminating" and laugh infrequently. (*Note:* Have you ever noticed people who laugh a lot while they're talking to you, but it isn't in response to anything humorous. Be careful not to confuse this nervous kind of laughter with a genuine appreciation of your humor.) This range is the typical composition of the audiences you will encounter. Put your material to the tougher test of gradually escalating the humor discrimination power of your testees. Try your successful level 1 material on a couple of "more discriminating" testees. They may provide a more realistic response to your humor, one that may match your class' response. Where you previously received cackles and, perhaps, a guffaw, now you may be in the smile to snicker range. Recall there are 15 possibilities in the stages of laughter (see Chapter 1), not including the "brain-dead" stare.

If you survived the level 2 testees, you're ready for small herds of testees, like several hovering over the coffee pot, bagels, and grits or those in a committee meeting. Use your best judgment to pick an appropriate group and, more importantly, an appropriate time; otherwise, you may be just shooting yourself in the spleen, or worse, at a meeting, possibly decapitating something to which you've really grown attached. If you have any doubts about who and when, don't do it. Wait for another opportunity that will give your material a fair test. A mixed reaction to the material by your little herd may be adequate.

It's time to test your material in class. Beware! Anything can happen! Positive responses at the previous stages of field testing may still not prepare you for the "class" reaction. Despite all of this preparation, you can still bomb. I know you will because I have bombed so many times with what I thought was great material that I stopped counting. It comes with the turf. Sometimes it is just very difficult to predict audience reactions to humorous material. I should also add that material that I thought would be met with a "moderate" response turned out to be a booming success with lots of laughter and applause occasionally. That just goes to show ya.

Chapter 4

Sources of Humorous Material

Where do you find ideas to create humor? You don't have to look far. The most unlimited source is your own imagination. To say that the ability to see and think humorously is a God-given gift is probably true. However, that really means God gave you a "twisted mind" to notice that third side of a coin and the incongruity in an ordinary situation. This does not preclude anyone else from learning to be twisted or from improving his or her twistedness. It just comes easier for some than for others, which occurs with all abilities. So how can you begin to generate your own funny material?

Analyze Who Makes You Laugh

Start with identifying a comic role model, a professional comedian, or just a friend who can keep you in stitches. Even if you consider yourself humorless, there must be somebody in the universe who can produce a smirk on your face or, perhaps, a chuckle. If you can't, GO BACK TO CHAPTER 1; DO NOT PASS GO, and DO NOT COLLECT $200. Get a life! If you have several favorite comics or humorists, that's even better. They could range from stand-up comics, such as Billy Crystal, Robin Williams, Steve Martin, Elayne Boosler, Mark Russell, Wolf Blitzer, and Joyce Brothers, to syndicated humor columnists Art

Buchwald, the late Erma Bombeck, Dave Barry, Fyodor Dostoevsky, and Flipper, to your cousins Moe, Larry, and Curly. What's important is that you find someone who makes you laugh.

Analyze What Makes You Laugh

Analyze why your role model(s) makes you hysterical. Is it the jokes themselves, the way they are told, or a combination of both. Sometimes it's difficult to differentiate. Not everyone can do accents and impersonations, which can be humorous no matter what is said. From this analysis, can you pinpoint the type of humor you find funny? Is it one-liners, put-downs, self-downs (self-effacing), satire, parody, impersonations, or several of those? Which types would you feel comfortable trying? Which ones fit your teaching style and personality best?

Be a student of humor. Study funny people to discover what they do that makes their humor successful — the content or form of the humor, their delivery (e.g., timing, body language), their voice, their physical appearance, their socks, etc. Experiment with *their* techniques to discover which ones you can perform effectively in front of your classes. Perret (1993) has noted that even professional comedians begin their careers by emulating comedians they admire; for example, Johnny Carson adopted the late Jack Benny's style and Robin Williams could be a reincarnation of Jonathan Winters. Of course, there are some who are simply unique, such as Rita Rudner, Paula Poundstone, Richard Pryor, Bill Cosby, Carrot Top, Gallagher, and Cokie Roberts.

Students represent a ready-made, captive, and sometimes willing training ground, albeit academic comedy club, for professorial attempts at humor. They are usually receptive and appreciate our efforts to make our subject matter more palatable and interesting. As your humor-writing and delivery skills improve with experience, your own comfortable style or brand of humor will emerge. Unlike professional comedians, however, in the course of completing your "humor bootcamp," you will have facilitated your effectiveness as a teacher and presenter with a substantive message, which is, "I'm here to entertain you. Nothing more, nothing less."

Read Humor Written by Others

There are tons of humor books on every type and form of jocularity described so far. In fact, I recall one entitled, *A Billion and One Jokes for All Occasions Except Bar Mitzvahs and College Teaching.* Just joshing! Whenever I accompany my two teenage daughters to the mall, as they shop for clothing they don't need, I can always be found browsing the latest humor acquisitions in the Walton's, Dalton's, or Abner Doubleday's Bookstore. It's great therapy even if I don't buy anything.

If you apply the "offensiveness" criteria listed in Chapter 3 to a typical bookstore humor-section inventory of 500 books, there would only be 6 or 7 books left to examine anyway. Although a few actually say *Truly Gross and Tasteless* ... on the cover, it takes about .02 nanoseconds to reach that conclusion about each of the others. This pervasive trend toward offensive humor also seems to be reflected in the available joke files on the Internet (see also Bell, Favale, & Kolin, 1996; Mayer, 1996).

One-liners, Top 10 Lists, and Anecdotes. Among the acceptable formats for low-risk humor illustrated in Chapter 3, quotation, multiple-choice, and top 10 jokes have one common denominator required for their construction — the one-liner. Another format was anecdotes. The following paperbacks can provide a truckload of ideas from which you can generate your own material and "adapt" (meaning to put your twisted spin) existing jokes to your content applications (a.k.a. platonic plagiarism):

One-liners

Andrews, B. L. (1994). *Digging your own grave.* New York: St. Martin's Press.

Anthony, M. Cagan, R., Light, L. & Power, A. (1993). *101 Reasons why we're doomed.* New York: Avon Books.

Becker, J., Mayer, A., & Maguire, B. (1994). *The 77 habits of highly ineffective people.* Kansas City, MO: Andrews and McMeel.

Biederman, J., & Biederman, L. M. (1996). *101 Ways to see the light: Near death experiences made simple.* New York: St. Martin's Press.

Bland, H., Falzarano, P., Niles, B., & Sears, M. (1993). *Life is too short.* New York: Warner Books.

Block, A. (1991). *The complete Murphy's Law: A definitive collection.* Los Angeles: Price Stern Sloan.

Byrne, R. (1988). *1,911 Best things anybody ever said.* New York: Fawcett Columbine.

Cader Company. (1996). *That's funny: A compendium of over 1,00 great jokes from today's hottest comedians.* New York: Cader Books (Andrews and McMeel).

Christing, A. (1996). *Comedy comes clean: A hilarious collection of wholesome jokes, quotes, and one-liners.* New York: Crown Trade Paperbacks.

Dane, C. S. (1992). *Life's little destruction book: A parody.* New York: St. Martin's Press.

Dane, C. S. (1993). *More life's little destruction book: A parody.* New York: St. Martin's Press.

Dickson, P. (1989). *The new official rules*. Reading, MA: Addison-Wesley.

Fechtner, L. (1986). *5000 One and two liners for any and every occasion*. Englewood Cliffs, NJ: Prentice-Hall.

Frankel, K., Wilson, R., & Salo, B. (1996). *Off the wall: The best graffiti off the walls of America*. Atlanta: Longstreet Press.

Fuller, E. (Ed.) (1994). *6200+ Wise cracks, witty remarks, and epigrams for all occasions*. Avenel, NJ: Wing Books (Random House Value Publishing).

Iapoce, M. (1988). *A funny thing happened on the way to the board room: Using humor in business speaking*. New York: Wiley.

Kipfer, B. A., & Strnad, E. (1996). *The optimist's/pessimist's guide to the millennium*. New York: Perigee Book (Berkley Publishing).

Lansky, B. (1996). *Age happens: The best quotes about growing older.* New York: Meadowbrook Press (Simon & Schuster).

Lapham, L. H., Pollan, M., & Etheridge, E. (1987). *The Harper's index book*. New York: Henry Holt and Company.

Loftin, G. (1994). *Grits for brains*. Asheboro, NC: Down Home Press.

Malloy, M. (1996). *Semi-deep thoughts*. New York: Pinnacle Books (Kensington Publishing).

Marsh, A. E., Blumenfield, J., & Moritz, R. (1995). *Sponging: A guide to living off those you love*. Venice, CA: Dune Road Books.

McTigue, G. G. (1994). *You know you're middle-aged when ...* New York: Pinnacle Books (Windsor Publishing).

O'Brien, T. (1995). *?* Newbury Park, CA: CCC Publications.

Perret, G. (1996). *Hilarious one-liners*. New York: Sterling Publishing.

Whaley, B. (1992). *Why the South lost the war ... and other things I don't understand*. Nashville, TN: Rutledge Hill Press.

Waldoks, M. (Ed). (1994). *The best American humor 1994*. New York: Touchstone (Simon & Schuster).

Top 10 Lists

Letterman, D., et al. (1990). *The "Late night with David Letterman" book of top ten lists*. New York: Pocket Books.

Letterman, D., et al. (1991). *An altogether new book of top ten lists*. New York: Pocket Books.

Letterman, D., et al. (1995). *David Letterman's book of top ten lists and zesty lo-cal chicken recipes*. New York: Bantam Books.

Letterman, D., et al. (1996). *David Letterman's new book of top ten lists and wedding dress patterns for the husky bride*. New York: Bantam Books.

Anecdotes

Adams, J. (1996). *Joey Adams' complete encyclopedia of laughter.* West Hollywood, CA: Dove Books.

Allen, S. (1987). *How to be funny: Discovering the comic in you.* New York: McGraw-Hill.

Asimov, I. (1971). *Isaac Asimov's treasury of humor.* Boston: Houghton Mifflin.

Iapoce, M. (1988). *A funny thing happened on the way to the board room: Using humor in business speaking.* New York: Wiley.

Pendleton, W. K. (1986a). *Complete speaker's galaxy of funny stories, jokes, and anecdotes.* Englewood Cliffs, NJ: Prentice-Hall.

Pendleton, W. K. (1986b). *Handbook of inspirational and motivational stories, anecdotes, and humor.* Englewood Cliffs, NJ: Prentice-Hall.

Readers Digest. (1996). *Life in these United States.* Pleasantville, NY: Readers Digest Association.

Waldoks, M. (Ed). (1994). *The best American humor 1994.* New York: Touchstone (Simon & Schuster).

Wright, R., & Wright, L. R. (1985). *500 Clean jokes and humorous stories and how to tell them.* Westwood, NJ: Barbour Books.

Cartoons and Riddles. These forms of humor can be found everywhere. Generic cartoons and riddles in books, newspapers, and popular magazines are so diverse that it becomes extremely time-consuming to select appropriate entries for professional presentations. Probably the best sources are the periodicals published within each discipline and association newsletters that occasionally present cartoons, riddles, and humorous crossword puzzles. Some of these sources are listed in Table 2. You might even find a text or workbook in your teaching area that has been written in the format of cartoons or riddles. There are actually two in my field of statistics:

Gonick, L., & Smith, W. (1993). *The cartoon guide to statistics.* New York: Harper Perennial.

Pyrczak, F. (1989). *Statistics with a sense of humor: A humorous workbook and guide to study skills.* Los Angeles: Fred Pyrczak.

Three cartoon books in medicine are listed below:

Booker, G. (Ed.). (1995). *Medicine is the best laughter.* St. Louis, MO: Mosby-Year Book.

Harris, S. (1994). *Stress test: Cartoons on medicine.* New Brunswick, NJ: Rutgers University Press.

New Yorker Magazine. (1993). *The New Yorker book of doctor cartoons.* New York: Alfred A. Knopf.

Table 2
Humor Journals, Magazines, and Newsletters

Journal/Newsletter	Editor	Address	Telephone
Humor Digest	Mack McGinnis	448 Mitchner Avenue Indianapolis, IN 46219	(317) 356-4616
Humor and Health Letter	Joe Richard Dunn	P.O. Box 16814 Jackson, MS 39236-6814	(601) 957-0075
Humor, Hypnosis, & Health Quarterly	Chuck Durham	CHUCKLE INSTITUTE P.O. Box 15462 Long Beach, CA 90815	
HUMOR: International Journal of Humor Research	Victor Raskin	Department of English Purdue University West Lafayette, IN 47907	(317) 494-3782
International Journal of Creature Communication	Charles Larson	Northern Illinois University Watson Hall 205 DeKalb, IL 60015	
Annals of Improbable Research (Journal of Irreproducible Results)	Marc Abrahams	Blackwell Scientific Publications Three Cambridge Center Cambridge, MA 02142	
Journal of Nursing Jocularity	Fran London	P.O. Box 40416 Mesa, AZ 85274	(602) 835-6165
Journal of Polymorphous Perversity	Glenn C. Ellenbogen	Wry-Bred Press, Inc P.O. Box 1454 New York, NY 10159-1454	
The Joyful Noiseletter	Cal and Rose Samra	The Fellowship of Merry Christians P.O. Box 668 Kalamazoo, MI 49005-0668	

Publication	Contact	Address	Phone
Just for Laughs	Hut Landon	22G Miller Avenue Mill Valley, CA 94941	
Knucklehead Press	Chris Miksanek Jim Riley	6442 West 111th Street Worth, IL 60482	
Latest Jokes	Robert Makinson	Box 3304 Brooklyn, NY 11202-0066	(718) 855-5057
Laughing Matters	Joel Goodman	110 Spring Street Saratoga Springs, NY 12866	
Laughlines	Ellie Marek	P.O. Box 32071 Phoenix, AZ 85064-2071	(602) 265-7010 (800) 253-3808
The Laughter Prescription Newsletter	Karen Silver	970 Shore Crest Road Carlsbad, CA 92009	(619) 931-6709
Laughter Works	Jim Pelley	P.O. Box 1076 Fair Oaks, CA 95628-1076	(916) 863-1592
The Onion	Scott Dikkers	33 University Square, Suite 270 Madison, WI 53715	(608) 256-1372
The Steve Wilson Report: Applying Psychology and Humor to Life and Work	Steve Wilson	3400 N. High Street Suite 120 Columbus, OH 43202	(800) NOW-LAFF
Stitches: The Journal of Medical Humor		14845 Younge St.,Suite 300 Aurora, Ontario Canada L4G 6H8	(800) 668-7412
Therapeutic Humor	Karyn Buxman	222 S. Meramec Dr., Suite 303 St. Louis, MO 63105	(314) 863-6232
Word Ways, The Journal of Recreational Linguistics	A. Ross Eckler	Spring Valley Road Morristown, NJ 07960	

Humorous Textbooks. There also may be textbooks in your discipline that are written humorously and/or use humorous illustrations and examples. In case you teach educational measurement and statistics, here are two by that dynamic duo of epidemiological comedians, Norman and Streiner, and two by my jocular mentor, Jim Popham:

Norman, G. R., & Streiner, D. L. (1994). *Biostatistics: The bare essentials.* St. Louis: Mosby.

Norman, G. R., & Streiner, D. L. (1997). *PDQ statistics* (2nd. ed.). St. Louis: Mosby.

Popham, W. J. (1990). *Modern educational measurement: A practitioner's perspective* (2nd ed.). Englewood Cliffs, NJ: Prentice Hall.

Popham, W. J. (1995). *Classroom assessment: What teachers need to know.* Needham Heights, MA: Allyn & Bacon.

Professional and Office Humor Books. Other sources of interest, though not as useful as the preceding, are several volumes that have been written on professional and office humor. They can suggest subjects that are fair game for humor as well as furnish many examples that may fit your needs.

Abrahams, M. (Ed.). (1993). *More of the best of the Journal of Irreproductible Results: Sex as a heap of malfunctioning rubble.* New York: Workman Publishing.

Baughman, M. D. (1974). *Baughman's handbook of humor in education.* Englewood Cliffs, NJ: Prentice-Hall.

Bennett, H. J. (Ed.). (1991). *The best of medical humor.* Philadelphia: Hanley & Belfus.

Block, A. (1991). *The complete Murphy's Law: A definitive collection.* Los Angeles: Price Stern Sloan.

Blumenfeld, E., & Alpern, L. (1994). *Humor at work.* Atlanta: Peachtree Publishers.

Davis, J. (1991). *Not the SAT.* New York: Dell Publishing.

Dickson, P. (1989). *The new official rules.* Reading, MA: Addison-Wesley.

Ellenbogen, G. C. (Ed.). (1989). *The primal whimper: More readings from the Journal of Polymorphous Perversity.* New York: Ballantine Books.

Fagan, P., & Schaffer, M. (1985). *The office humor book.* New York: Harmony Books.

Fagan, P., & Schaffer, M. (1992). *Office humor II.* New York: Harmony Books.

Faxenmoff, I. (1994). *Fax-ready guerrilla grams.* Los Angeles: Corkscrew Press.

Hirsch, M. E. (Ed.) (1995). *A treasury of office humor.* Springfield, IL: Lincoln- Herndon Press.

Iggers, J. (1991). *Off the office wall.* Stanford, CT: Longmeadow Press.

Kanter, A., & Kanter, J. (1995). *The lawyer's big book of fun.* Chicago: Contemporary Books.

Kenefick, C., & Young, A. Y. (1993). *The best of nursing humor.* Philadelphia: Hanley & Belfus.

London, O. (1987). *Kill as few patients as possible.* Berkeley, CA: Ten Speed Press.

London, O. (1989). *Take one as needed.* Berkeley, CA: Ten Speed Press.

Myers, J. E. (Ed.). (1993). *A treasury of medical humor.* Springfield, IL: Lincoln- Herndon Press.

Myers, J. E. (Ed.). (1996). *A treasury of business humor.* Springfield, IL: Lincoln- Herndon Press.

Paulos, J. A. (1982). *Mathematics and humor.* Chicago: University of Chicago Press.

Scherr, G. H. (Ed.). (1983). *The best of the Journal of Irreproductible Results.* New York: Workman Publishing.

Schroeder, N., & Mintzer, R. (1986). *The unofficial nurse's handbook.* New York: Plume Book (Penguin Books).

Susan, P., & Mamchak, S. R. (1987). *Encyclopedia of school humor: Icebreakers, classics, stories, puns, and roasts for all occasions.* Englewood Cliffs, NJ: Prentice-Hall.

Warlock, A. (1990). *250 Funniest office jokes, memos and cartoon pinups.* Collinsville, IL: Knightraven Books.

Warlock, A. (1995). *250 Funniest office jokes, memos, and cartoon pinups (Vol. 2).* Collinsville, IL: Knightraven Books.

Weller, T. (1987). *Culture made stupid.* Boston: Houghton Mifflin.

Zevin, D. (1994). *Entry-level life: A complete guide to masquerading as a member of the real world.* New York: Bantam Books.

Humor Journals, Magazines, and Newsletters. As mentioned previously, there are also a variety of humor journals, magazines, and newsletters that publish generic and professional humor. They are listed in Table 2. Some of these may be available on the Internet.

As you peruse all of these sources, jot down specific ideas and topics and gather quotes, jokes, stories, cartoons, etc. that are appropriate for your teaching and other presentations. Start a humor file of possible material from which you can draw content to build jokes for particular applications.

Music Sources for Skits. Finally, there is no collection of sources for humorous skits or dramatizations for college teaching, although there is one book by Flacks and Raspberry (1982) that provides numerous theatrical techniques for speakers. However, music is such an integral component of the skits I have tested, it may be a useful starting point. Current television and movie themes can be recorded directly from the original medium with a tape deck or CD player or purchased in your local music store. Older as well as more recent themes from television series of the '50s through the '90s can be obtained from 10 CDs:

Television's Greatest Hits, Vol. 1 (65 TV themes from the 50's & 60's) — Tee Vee Toons (TVT 1100CD)

Television's Greatest Hits, Vol. II (65 More TV themes from the 50's & 60's) — Tee Vee Toons (TVT 1200CD)

Television's Greatest Hits 70's & 80's, Vol. 3 (65 More of your favorite TV themes) — Tee Vee Toons (TVT 1300CD)

Television's Greatest Hits: Black & White Classics, Vol. 4 (65 TV themes from the 50's & 60's) — Tee Vee Toons (TVT 1600CD)

Television's Greatest Hits in Living Color, Vol. 5 (65 TV themes from the 60's & 70's) — Tee Vee Toons (TVT 1700-2CD)

Television's Greatest Hits Remote Control, Vol. 6 (65 TV themes from the 70's & 80's) — Tee Vee Toons (TVT 1800CD)

Television's Greatest Hits Cable Ready, Vol. 7 (65 TV themes from the 80's & 90's) — Tee Vee Toons (TVT 1900-2CD)

Rhino Tube Tunes, Vol. 1, the '70s (R2 71910CD)

Rhino Tube Tunes, Vol. 2, the '70s & '80s (R2 71911CD)

Rhino Tube Tunes, Vol. 3, the '80s (R2 71912CD)

Observe Humor Around You

Once you are in humor mode, you will begin to notice a humorous angle or element in the most mundane, everyday situations. Search for humor in everything you do in the office, especially in what you read and what you write. Some of the policies and procedures we're requested to follow and the memos, e-mail, reports, and other communication vehicles can be a riot if we look at them from a jocular perspective. Notice humor in your conversations with students, faculty, secretaries, administrators, and parole officers. Sitting in meetings can become a new mirthful event. (Yeah, right!) Try having an out-of-meeting experience while sitting in the meeting; that is, remove yourself mentally for a little while, as you've probably done many times, but instead of drifting, observe your peers in action. It's amazing how comical colleagues can be when they're super-serious and obsessed about an issue.

Record stories you hear and humorous ideas that just pop out from what you observe. Think about writing humorous agendas for meetings and office memos, injecting humor into meeting minutes (that's a sure-fire way of never being asked to take minutes again), and bringing some levity into the trillion committee, departmental, school, and university-wide meetings you attend. Your humorous observations can also be transformed into multiple-choice and top 10 formats for professional presentations. Consider the topics of memos, meetings, and committees and review some of my examples in Chapters 2, 3, and 8.

Chapter 5

Delivering Humor Effectively

Step-by-step procedures for delivering specific forms of humor were presented in Chapter 3. This chapter examines the major techniques for delivering humor to maximize its laughter potential in your classes and in any professional presentation. The goal of your delivery should be to appear natural, spontaneous, expressive, and hilarious. That requires hours of practice and rehearsal, just like a Broadway performance. Since the humor is being used as a teaching tool, it must be able to generate and maintain the interest, attention, and involvement of your audience. The recommendations that follow address various methods for producing that type of impact. Experience tells us that good and even brilliant humorous material can fall flat without effective delivery. No one wants to "bomb." In humor, the secret to success is great material, a dynamite delivery, and Whoopi Goldberg's agent.

It has been estimated that people remember:

10% of what they hear,

30% of what they see,

60% of what they hear and see,

80% of what they hear, see, and do, and

100% of what they hear, see, do, smell, feel, taste, inhale, inject, and purchase on credit.

Although that 100% goal is impressive, it would be impractical and probably illegal to attain instructionally in our classrooms. The 80% phrase is a more realistic instructional formula. It translates our delivery into verbal and nonverbal components and, if possible, a mechanism for providing our students with the opportunity to participate. This element of participation is an essential ingredient in many of the strategies currently being used in active learning, cooperative and collaborative learning, critical thinking, and applications of the latest technologies. As you use humor as a teaching tool, strive to incorporate participation and as many of those components as possible into your delivery. This effort should result in a "memorable" performance.

WARNING: This next paragraph is really cerebral. So hold on to your Gore-Tex. Here we go.

Underlying these elements of learning is your ability to integrate right brain and left brain functions. The right hemisphere controls visual and spatial abilities, intuitive feelings, and perceptual insight. It is the creative and physically expressive side. The left hemisphere controls speech and the higher order functions of the nervous system, including the intellect and complex perceptual processes. In other words, it is the source of our language functions and mental skills. (*Semi-Deep Thought:* According to Marie Kelley, "If the left side of the brain controls the right side of the body, then only left-handed people are in their right mind!" Right?)

Delivering humor effectively requires that you draw from all of your available resources, mental and physical, so that you are an audiovisual demonstration of your own material. (Admittedly, some of you have more resources to draw on than others.) Your words plus your physical expressiveness in your eyes, face, hands and arms, and the rest of your body can create an unforgettable image. Consider for a moment the memorable image of a taxi driver directing other drivers by using only eyeballs, incisors, nostrils, spit, one finger, and knuckles. You too can be just as dramatic in your classroom. Further, if you can involve your students in the course of your delivery by requesting them to speak, write, or move, the impact can be even stronger.

As professors, you are probably already using these methods in your teaching. Your lectures may be very expressive, your illustrations utilize a variety of audiovisual aids, you regularly force your students to perform what you demonstrate, and you use gestures to assist other drivers in traffic. These effective teaching strategies can be adapted to the delivery of your humor.

The remainder of this chapter presents 14 recommendations for improving the effectiveness of your delivery, including specific guidelines for selecting and using audiovisual aids. (*Note:* Most of these recommendations are applicable to the delivery of lectures and

professional presentations as well as humor.) As you process these recommendations and apply them to your delivery, study the delivery of
your favorite humorists and comedians as role models. When you see
them perform, concentrate on their word choice, timing, voice modulation and intonation, diction, and body language and movement.
Watch how they create an atmosphere that is conducive to laughter.
For example, notice Jerry Seinfeld's timing, Billy Crystal's intonation,
Lily Tomlin's, Bill Cosby's, and Jim Carrey's facial expressions, Robin
Williams' gestures, Steve Martin's body language, and Jack Palance's
one-arm push-ups.

Pre-Delivery Preparation

Your pre-delivery preparation begins with one final maintenance
check on the images you will create with your words. Make sure you
select not only what you deem to be the most appropriate words for
your humor, but also graphic and colorful (not in the "offensive"
sense) words and expressions to paint a vivid funny picture in the
minds of your audience. Such words create an emotional linkage with
the audience. It has been said that "There can be an enormous difference between the right word and the nearly right word."

Previously the structure and wording of several forms of humor
were described and illustrated (see Chapters 2 and 3). The sudden
shift from the expected and usually "serious" element to the unexpected twist or punch line hinges on the right words. It was noted that
humor is a function of the picture you create with those words. The
skillful choice of words will produce strong images that, in turn, generate the humor. Visualize the humorous material you have written. Is
it funny because it conjures up a ridiculous image? For example, take
a realistic, unfunny image and twist, distort, or exaggerate it totally out
of proportion to be able to visualize a funny new image. The more
exaggerated, absurd, and bizarre the image seems in the imagination
of your audience, the more effective the humor and the greater the
laughter. Perret (1982a) emphasized that a "joke is not the collection
of words; it's the scene that appears in the listener's mind as a result of
those words" (p. 61). Consider how the following Dave Barry expressions create funny mental pictures:

- The Official State Bird of Alaska is covered with oil. (Barry, 1991,
  p. 68)
- He is as organized as a tub of live bait. (Barry, 1989, p. 151)
- That fact will forever remain a large stone lodged in the kidney of
  my memory. (Barry, 1988, p. 260)
- The leading cause of death among fashion models is falling
  through street grates. (Barry, 1988, p. 165)

- Drivers who are not passing, squatting in the left lane, are little globules of fat clogging up the transportation arteries of our very nation. (Barry, 1988, p. 209)
- I would rather undergo a vasectomy via Weed Wacker than attend an opera. (Barry, 1991, p. 147)
- Mr. Jack O' Lantern immediately gets his face kicked into mush by older youngsters playing pranks. (Barry, 1991, p. 153)
- You'll wind up bobbing helplessly in the water while sharks chew on your legs as if they were a pair of giant Slim Jims. (Barry, 1994, p. 110)

Graphic words, hyperboles, and figurative language, such as similes and metaphors, can create the ridiculous image that produces the humor.

The effectiveness of your delivery begins here. It is a function of the image you create from words and how you create it. Scrutinize all of your humorous material according to this "funny image" criterion. Revise or discard material that doesn't measure up. There is no point in spending a lot of time to practice your delivery of material that doesn't deliver. Polish the wording in your material to make every word and phrase count in your delivery of the image you want the audience to visualize.

Memorize Your Material

Memorize the final version of your humorous material. Practice it until it doesn't sound memorized. High-risk stand-up jokes and low-risk anecdotes can not be read to your audience. Actually they can be, just that you'll be digging your own tar pit. It's about as effective as sucking a Brunswick bowling ball through a straw. The only thing that happens is the veins in your forehead pop out and eventually explode. Successful delivery of those forms of humor requires memorization to a level that makes your delivery look so natural, albeit conversational, that it would appear as though you're just telling the joke to a friend or even your mother, assuming you're on good joke-telling terms.

The audience should see you as relaxed, informal, and even folksy, possibly heavily sedated, but never comatose, especially in your delivery of an anecdote. How else can the joke create those feelings in your audience if you don't convey those feelings yourself. Your demeanor or the tone you set for the joke should contrast to some degree with the delivery style of your serious message. The humor is intended to inject a break or change of pace in what otherwise may be the dull and boring substance of your lecture or presentation. This is not to suggest that you create the opposite emotional effect with the substantive part by standing at attention like George C. Scott and transmitting tension instead of relaxation. (*Pop Quiz:* What does the "C" stand for? *Hint:*

Helga.) You should appear comfortable, relaxed, and in complete control throughout your entire presentation.

The other forms of low-risk humor that are displayed on overheads or slides do not need to be memorized. However, you should be so familiar with that material that it almost looks memorized. Although you will "read" the humor as the audience reads it, it must be practiced so many times that you can maintain eye contact with the audience as you deliver each line. If the way you deliver the quotations, captions on the cartoons, multiple-choice items, and top 10 lists does not enhance the impact of the humor, then don't bother reading the material. Sing it instead. Ha ha! In fact, you can experiment in your classes by presenting the material visually only, and then by combining the visual display with your oral delivery. The increment in laughter produced by the latter can justify the visual-oral combo approach. You're probably thinking, "How can I accurately measure the laughter from my humor?" May I suggest the new RONco Laugh-O-Meter®, available only from my publisher for $19.95, plus $5.05 for shipping and fondling. Also, for a limited time, 12,000 miles, or until next millennium, whichever comes first, they will include a Ginsu razor-sharp indestructible butcher knife, just like the one Michael Myers used in *Halloween XIII* to slice and dice the entire cast. I know you'll think of some use for it such as slicing off increments or shredding this book. (Now wasn't that semi-jocular break refreshing? I think it's time to get back to our story about modes and components.)

I have discovered that cartoons, pictures, tables, and graphs very often work better in visual mode only or that my delivery of the visual component really doesn't contribute that much to the impact. However, even with these forms of humor, you may want to read the verbal content to control the pace of your presentation. If *you* read it, you're ready to move on; if the *audience* reads it, you may be uncertain when to move on. Your only obvious cue to proceed is when the laughter subsides. With little or no laughter, it's difficult to judge how long to wait for the audience to read and process the material. Moss growing on the edges of your transparency is usually a sign that it's time to get on with your life.

Practice Your Timing

The pause of a couple of seconds that precedes the punch line in virtually all forms of humor must be perfectly timed to allow the tension to peak. The timing in your delivery of verbal material is critical to the effectiveness of the humor. In your oral presentation of the material mentioned above, it can be the timing in the way you interpret the multiple-choice item, for example, that makes it funnier than just relying on the audience's reading. You can create the edge to improve the impact of your material by controlling the build-up of tension with strategically placed pauses. In other words, you need to practice pausing or saying nothing at key points in your delivery. As professors, "saying nothing" is not one of our strengths. That will probably require statistically significant amounts of will power. Even mediocre material that can elicit a so-so response when simply read by the audience can be transformed to produce a spectacular response when it is delivered with the proper timing.

How do you know when to pause and for how long? Here are four hints:

1. Dissect the structure of your material to pinpoint the punch line. (This is almost the same as dissecting a frog to identify the glop.)

2. As you practice the delivery, lead up to the punch slowly, but with authority, to allow your audience to absorb the first element and to create anticipation of the punch line. The first serious part of a quotation, the stem in a multiple-choice item, and the lead-in to a top 10 list are designed expressly to build the tension in the audience. Don't zoom through this element to get to the punch line.

3. Once you sense the tension has peaked at the point in your material just before the punch, STOP! Pause for a moment or two. Let the audience suffer in anticipation of what's coming. Suspend them in mid air. Torture them by not saying the punch line immediately. Try to enter their minds to gauge when they are ready for the punch.

4. After you have finished playing with your audience's minds, deliver the punch line forcefully and dramatically. This will release all of their tension, optimistically in the form of convulsive laughter.

If you begin to receive this response to your humorous material by your students with unusual regularity, you might want to consider a career change. Consistent responses in the "guffaw" to "die laughing" range strongly indicate you have professional comedy potential.

Involve Your Audience

Active participation in your humor jolts your students or audience into attentiveness. This effect can also be obtained electrically or with the Heimlich maneuver, although with a little less laughter. If possible, during your delivery, solicit their involvement. One simple method is to just ask questions, such as one that requires a verbal response. For example, the *Home Improvement* skit requests the audience to answer: "What time is it?" Because it's totally unexpected, their first response is uneven. Giving them a second chance to redeem themselves gets them revved up. Their second response is thunderous. They are now part of the action and a participant in the skit.

Another technique is to ask your audience one or more questions on a particular topic that requires them to raise their hands. This minimal physical response forces them to become participants. These questions can be asked prior to a joke to peak their attention to receive the humor or during your presentation periodically to retrieve wandering minds, wake-up the sleepers, and to maintain the interest and attention of those who are listening. Examples of these questions are given for specific classroom and presentation applications in the next two chapters.

Finally, written responses, other than note-taking, can sustain involvement in your presentation. Presenting a humorous quiz, rating scale, or puzzle can have the same effects as the handraising. Further, it can be administered in a variety of forms at the beginning, throughout, and at the end of any message. Examples of a quiz, rating scale, and *Jeopardy!* type review for exams are described in Chapter 6. (Also see *Jeopardy!* quiz in Chapter 7.)

Whatever technique you choose to involve your audience, make sure the response is easy and nonthreatening. The most effective methods require the audience to speak, shout, write, raise their hands, stand, or smack the person next to them, usually with a blunt instrument. Any method that requests a response that's more strenuous or intimidating than those is doomed to failure. If the audience is asked to perform a task that may be silly, embarrassing, difficult, degrading, or stupid, they probably won't do it, plus, when you're finished, they'll throw frozen vegetables at you.

Vary Your Voice Modulation, Intonation, and Speed

Since the "deadly" monotone speaker we've all heard too many times probably represents the worst form of delivery, any variation in your voice would be an improvement. Unfortunately, "any variation" in the delivery of humor is totally unacceptable. As the preceding sections indicate, your voice modulation, tone, and speed must be deliberate and executed perfectly to maximize the impact of your humor.

Your volume must be loud enough so that everyone can hear every word. Speaking softly may be appropriate when groveling before your dean, but it can kill your humor. You should project at the same level as an actor on stage. The only differences are in the scripts, costumes, makeup, work hours, dressing room, benefits packages, and paychecks. For example, you are performing your words, not a role written by someone else, and James Earl Jones and Emma Thompson on Broadway would be compensated in one month what most junior faculty receive in a year.

However, I think we're off on a tangent and need a sine back to the subject of this paragraph, which is a little trigonometric humor. Depending on the size of your classrooms, you should adjust your volume accordingly. When microphones are available for presentations in auditoriums, ballrooms, theater-style lecture halls, and football stadiums, don't scream at your usual classroom volume. (After 25 years of teaching, I seem to talk too loudly all the time because of my classroom conditioning.)

As you deliver your humorous material, vary your voice level between the lead-in serious element and the punch line. As you practice the different formats, use your volume to build tension before the punch. In an anecdote, create feeling and drama during the course of your story by increasing and decreasing your volume at appropriate points. The higher volume adds emphasis and, therefore, should coincide with the most important lines, especially the punch line. Simply modulating your voice level can maintain your audience's attention and increase their tension during your delivery to contribute to the impact of your humor. It can also improve the effectiveness of your delivery by portraying the impression of power and confidence.

Tone can be manipulated as easily as your voice level to increase the effectiveness of your delivery. As noted previously, the tone should match the form of the humor. Anecdotes should be told conversationally. One-liners such as quotations and questions, multiple-choice items, and top 10 lists should be presented forcefully.

The previous section emphasized the role of speed of delivery in building tension and in the timing of the punch line. Control the speed of your delivery by establishing a rhythm for each form of humor. The rhythm for a one-liner is very different from that of a multiple-choice item. Be consistent in your rhythm throughout a series of jokes in the same format, similar to the rhythm of the Radio City Rockettes' kick line or Green Bay Packers' offensive line. Blumenfeld and Alpern (1994) stress that the rhythm of your delivery is "maintained by your pace and supported by the momentum of accelerating anticipation" (p. 93). The audience is primed by the rhythm you set. Take advantage of their anticipation in the timing of your delivery.

Enunciate Every Word

Mumbling, garbling, slurring, spitting, or drooling your words is a bit off the beaten path to successful delivery of humor, and, eventually, stardom and your own sitcom. Any one of those behaviors can result in the immediate and painful death of your humor. Welcome to BOMBSville! Once you've blown the delivery, it's over. There is no way to save the joke.

It is absolutely essential that you speak clearly and precisely. Remember every word counts and contributes to the success of your humor. The audience should not have to strain their eardrums to understand you. Certainly their position in the room should not affect their ability to hear every word. In fact, they should be able to easily process what you say as well as be sensitive to your voice modulation, intonation, and speed to realize the full impact of your humorous material.

Use Facial Expressions

We have all encountered super-serious, cadaver-like colleagues with the emotional range of formica. Your facial expressions communicate feelings and emotions that can be used to animate your humor. Consider how the late Jack Benny's and Johnny Carson's stare directly into the audience's eyes could produce laughter by itself. Jim Carrey creates hysteria by contorting his rubber-like face into bizarre expressions. (*Friendly Advice:* While we're on the subject of Jim Carrey's nose, I suggest you AVOID sticking objects in yours, such as asparagus, tree limbs, and exhaust pipes, and using "boogers" in any joke intended for students and professional audiences.) These examples illustrate the extremes on a continuum of how you can use your face to bring your humor to life.

The best method to test different facial expressions as you deliver humorous material is in front of a mirror. If you don't like the expressions you see, you might consider wearing a mask or having plastic surgery. If you don't see any image in the mirror, then you should immediately call the Vampire Hot Line (1-900-TOM-CRUISE). The expressions should match the content of the material and appear natural. When you reach any punch line, make sure to keep a straight face to build suspense until it's complete. Otherwise, your eyes or the smirk on your face could interfere with the build-up of tension or telegraph the punch is coming.

Gesture With Your Hands and Arms

Gestures are a natural part of our communicative repertoire (literally means "talk to your toire") when we feel comfortable, relaxed, and uninhibited in our conversation with someone. Everyone gestures, just that some people gesticulate more than others and with different styles, especially taxi drivers from second world countries, such as Okra. We instinctively rely on our gestures to communicate our words.

Since a "talking head" hiding behind a lectern is gestureless and, coincidentally super-boring, the more pronounced your body language, the greater chance you have of keeping the attention of your audience. Body movement, in general, and gestures, in particular create a sense of animation and vitality. They say to the audience: "I'm alive! "I'm not dead yet, and even if I was, I wouldn't let you bury me!"

Delivering your humor with appropriately-timed hand movements can add emphasis, drama, and energy, thereby, increasing its impact. For classroom use with 20 to 100 students, hand gestures can usually be seen easily; for audiences of a few hundred to the size of Iraq, use full arm gestures and nuclear weapons for greater effect (small movements and handguns do not project as well).

As with every other aspect of your delivery, practice your gestures until they feel natural. Analyze their visual effect by performing your material in front of a mirror. (Wow! This is like *Groundhog Day*. I'm experiencing "vichyssoise," pronounced, "Ver-SIGH.") Determine whether they actually look as natural as they feel or whether they seem artificial or forced. Do they fit the verbal content of the joke appropriately? For example, are the gestures timed to emphasize the punch line or do they telegraph inappropriately that the punch is coming? Regular use of gestures helps you become the best audiovisual you can be and the focal point of your presentation. The audiovisual image you create keeps the audience's eyes, teeth, lungs, and bladders riveted on you. Using your entire body amplifies this image even more.

Move Your Body Around

When you move all over the room or stage, your students or audience have to keep their eyes glued on you. They are forced to follow the action; they don't know where you're going or what you're going to do next. Your movement generates dynamic tension, energy, excitement, and terror, which keeps your audience alert. It also expresses your enthusiasm for your humor and the content to be presented, and reduces any anxiety or stress you may feel because you're actually engaging in exercise.

In contrast to these benefits of body movement, what are the effects of being planted into the floor like Rocky in his first movie? The first effect is you're gonna get whupped by Apollo Creed. Oops, we're off the subject again. If you're standing frozen like a glacier behind a lectern or on the side of an overhead projector, you are in danger of exhibiting "talking-head syndrome" or THS. (*Medical Tip:* THS can be treated with one precisely administered dose of the revolutionary French medication, Guillotinac. It permanently cures THS.) THS means that although you may not be brain-dead yet, you are "body dead" and your audience is probably on their way to join you. If you convey the image of being on life support, your audience can be expected to produce a similar response to your humor. They may appear solemn and even deceased. Even worse than stand-up rigor mortis-style humor is presenting jokes while sitting down or prostrate. If you're sitting at a conference table for a seminar or meeting, your students' or colleagues' eyes are more likely to close than stay glued on you while your talking. A static delivery, either standing or sitting, produces a listless, creepy, and eventually, dead audience.

Delivering your humor effectively requires that you incorporate every visual resource at your disposal to render the impact not only funny but memorable. In other words, "let your body do the talking." Robin Williams creates "electricity" on stage as he romps everywhere to express his humor physically as well as mentally. Humor is a dynamic, integrated right brain/left brain exercise. Use your entire body as a communicative instrument for your humor.

Among the forms of humor described in Chapter 3, the skit/dramatization provides the most expressive vehicle to combine mental and physical activities. The *Home Improvement* skit has had the strongest impact on my classes and professional audiences of any humor strategy I have ever attempted. I try to create an unforgettable image with the metaphor of tools plus the visual impact of actual screwdrivers, hammer and drill, the toolbelt, yellow suspenders, small and large gestures with the tools, transparencies, audience participation, moving around the classroom or stage as I'm talking, and theme music. Almost every student and peer who has seen both the *Home Improvement* and *Mister Rogers'* skits comment that the former is much more powerful than the latter. Why? Compared to "Tool Man," Mister Researcher utilizes fewer props, much less body movement, no talking, and no audience participation. It is essentially a pantomime and the whole tone is lower key and subdued.

Body movement and language should not be restricted to the front of the room. Move into your audience, down the aisles, around the sides and back of the room, into every nook and crevice. Remember they have to watch your every move. Circulating among your students as you are telling a joke or anecdote builds a sense of closeness, intimacy, and fear. It eliminates the physical as well as psychological distance between you and your class. Further, you are demonstrating an interest in them by lavishing attention on everyone in the room, not just the few who sit in the front. It gives them a feeling of participation and involvement in your humor and everything else you have to say.

In presentations to large audiences, such as Madonna speaking to Argentina, use a wireless lavaliere microphone to provide flexibility of movement on the stage or podium and to allow you to move closer to your audience. Move away from the lectern and overhead projector when you're not using it. Depending on the seating arrangement, you might be able to walk around in the aisles. In addition to the advantages mentioned above, physical closeness to your audience helps build a rapport and intimate connection that creates a psychological closeness. Members of your audience view you as stepping off your pedestal, eliminating the distance, and coming down to be with us, or even to be like us. You might recall that every evening after Johnny Carson stepped out from behind the curtain to begin his monologue, he would move to a specific premarked position on the stage and remained there the entire time. When Jay Leno took over the *Tonight Show,* he had a special small stage extension built into the front section of the audience at a lower level than the original stage. The sole purpose was to increase his closeness to the audience and provide an intimacy typically found in small comedy clubs. During the monologue, Leno moves all over that tiny stage with dramatic facial expressions and gestures to create a strong visual image.

> **WARNING:** This next section is the high-tech part of the book. The novice professor is forewarned that sophisticated, electronic-type jargon will be used in these paragraphs. Be prepared to tackle technical words, such as on, off, chalk, bulb, over, head, burns out, stuck, play, and reverse. Proceed at your own risk.

Use Audiovisual Aids

The goo running through the preceding five recommendations for improving your delivery is: *YOU are the best audiovisual there is.* You're a "live dramatization" of your humor. Take advantage of your voice and visual appearance to capture and maintain the eyes, ears, nose, and throat of your audience. And, unlike other audiovisuals, you probably won't burn out, crash, flicker, darken, jam-up, break down, blast feedback, fall off the wall, or die, at least not in front of your students.

All other audiovisuals are simply aids or props, secondary to you. Why should they be used in the presentation of humor? Because I said so! As noted at the beginning of this chapter, the delivery of humor can have a greater impact on an audience when they are forced to integrate both right brain and left brain functions than when they use only one function. Instead of presenting some of the forms of humor verbally or visually, you are strongly encouraged to use the combination to appeal to both sides of your listeners' minds. Audiovisuals can increase their interest, attention, and involvement, plus help create pictures with the words you use, which is a key element in the effectiveness of humor.

Any equipment you choose should be based on its characteristics to support you, to complement your performance, and to facilitate the delivery of your humorous material as well as the substance of your message. Almost every humor strategy described in this book utilizes audiovisuals, especially an overhead projector, to deliver the material effectively. In fact, step-by-step procedures for presenting several forms of humor in Chapters 3, 5, and 6 were listed. This section examines some of the advantages and disadvantages of the chalkboard (or white board), overhead projector, slide projector, computer, tape player, and simple props, such as a boa constrictor, chain saw, and canoe. The rule of thumb that should guide your choice of these aids is: Keep it simple; otherwise the aids can become the main attraction and center of the audience's attention and you become the aid.

Chalkboard (or White Board). The chalkboard is the most widely used and oldest visual aid in classrooms everywhere. In fact, its origin dates back to prehistoric times when parents like Fred and Wilma Flintstone homeschooled their daughter Pebbles by using the cave walls as a chalkboard. Unfortunately, its use as an instructional aid was limited because English had not been invented yet. However, its value as an aid for presenting humor is even more restricted. This assessment of the chalkboard also applies to the more recent white board, which uses a liquid chalk marker or washable felt marker instead of the traditional dry, "dustless," stick-in-the-nostrils-and-lungs chalk.

Considering the various forms of humor appropriate for your classroom use, writing any joke on the chalkboard does not permit you to control the build-up of tension which is an essential ingredient for success. However, it does allow for the element of surprise. A joke, quotation, proverb, multiple-choice item, or top 10 list can be written on the board and covered with a ceiling projector screen before the students arrive. As the opening joke in class, it can be revealed by retracting the screen. You can read it aloud as your students read it silently or it can be presented just as a visual. For one-liner jokes, quotations, and proverbs, the chalkboard can work, assuming every student can read anything on the board easily from their positions in the room. Students in the back and far sides usually need high-powered binoculars and have difficulty deciphering my jocular doodles. The formats that contain more than one line and require the gradual build-up of tension can be delivered more effectively on an overhead projector. Their impact will be significantly diminished on the chalkboard. A further limitation is that due to the relatively small hand lettering required for the standard-size chalkboard, it would be impossible to use it as an aid in large rooms.

Overhead Projector. Among the types of electronic visual aids available, the overhead projector is by far the most popular for classroom, meeting room, and large presentation room applications. I suspect that your years of teaching experience has led you to conclude that it has the following advantages as an instructional aid:

(1) it is easy to operate,

(2) it is highly dependable,

(3) it has a spare bulb built in for immediate use should one burn out,

(4) it can be used in any size room as long as an appropriate size screen is available,

(5) it can be operated effectively in a fully lighted room to permit eye contact and note taking,

(6) it allows you to face your audience to maintain eye contact and to watch for cues and reactions,

(7) it can be easily turned on or off to focus attention on you or the screen,

(8) it permits you flexibility of movement around the room when it's not in use,

(9) it allows you control over exactly what your audience sees through the "revelation" method of bits and pieces of information,

(10) transparencies can be removed or changed at the last minute or during a presentation easily should the humor be considered inappropriate for any reason (see Chapter 7),

(11) attractive, colorful, eye-catching, designer transparencies of any verbal, graphic, or pictorial content can be produced quickly and inexpensively,

(12) it allows you to be creative with shadow puppets when all else fails, and

(13) it can be used as a stage spotlight by adjusting the projection mirror to simulate a live performance of your stand-up comedy or song and dance routine.

I have the feeling you're thinking, "Ron, thanks for sharing that list, but I already know that stuff. Heeelloo! I've been using an overhead since the Civil War!" Well, Bucko (or Buckette), which of those attributes are most valuable as aids in presenting humorous material? Huh? Huh? The recommendations for effective delivery discussed in this chapter suggest that advantages (5), (6), (7), (8), and (10) are extremely important for audience interest, attention, involvement, and visual impact. However, the one advantage that is absolutely critical to deliver most forms of humor successfully is (14). (Just checking if you're still awake.) Step-by-step renditions of the revelation method (9) were given for several humor formats in Chapter 3. The ability to control the timing of the delivery from beginning to end is essential. A transparency with a blank sheet of paper on top or under it is the simplest and most effective aid to execute that timing, especially the build-up of tension, in conjunction with the ease of observing your audience for cues in that process. Although a set of overlays can serve the same purpose, it is less efficient and more complicated to construct.

Slide Projector. The slide projector has become a very useful instructional aid in the areas of business and health (which have congealed into a mammoth empire) where slides of financial information and photographs can be displayed effectively. Unfortunately, it is not as applicable to the content in other fields, particularly for classroom use. Compared to the overhead, its disadvantages outweigh its advantages by a whopping margin. Those disadvantages include:

(1) lower level of dependability with slides getting stuck,

(2) spare bulb cannot be easily replaced if one burns out,

(3) room has to be completely darkened, which precludes seeing the audience at all, much less eye contact, note taking, and your movement around the room,

(4) turning it on or off is inconvenient because it's usually positioned out in the audience,

(5) requires several slides compared to one transparency to use the revelation method,

(6) slides cannot be removed from the carousel or changed at the last minute or during a presentation should the humorous material be judged inappropriate for any reason, and

(7) slides are time-consuming and expensive to produce.

These seven disadvantages render the slide projector as less useful than the overhead projector for the forms of humor described in this book.

However, a unique advantage of slides as a visual aid is in the presentation of humorous photographs on any subject. As a change of pace, such a segment illustrating a serious point humorously can be very effective. The lecture or presentation could also employ the overhead for other humor formats.

Computer. Multimedia classroom and conference presentations using computers are increasing nationwide, particularly at community and liberal arts colleges. Unfortunately, the technology is still not available everywhere. A computerized presentation of several of the humor formats described previously could be given in lieu of overhead transparencies. PowerPoint affords the control needed for delivering one line at a time using a laptop computer and LED box. If an entire presentation is computerized, the humor can be automatically incorporated. The use of the computer for delivering just the humor would probably not be justified. Further, the complexity of a multimedia high-tech presentation may produce technical problems that could destroy the execution of the humor. It's tough enough to control the build-up of tension and timing of the punch without encountering the glitch of a lost punch, the wrong line, or another error in delivery. It is advisable to have a back-up set of transparencies available in case of any technical problems which can occur in a class or conference presentation.

Tape Player. A small tape player (about 5"x 7") is an efficient and effective audio aid to produce your own musical accompaniment for skits and dramatizations without depending on on-site audiovisual capabilities and a technician. Although the sound is not Carnegie Hall quality, the result is more than adequate compared to relying on someone else's sound system. If you need to play two or more tapes during your presentation, it is recommended that you have at least two of those small players prepared with the cassettes loaded so you don't have to fumble trying to unload and load cassettes as you're speaking. This recommendation is derived from my numerous encounters with "Murphy's Law" of cassette loading.

Props. The specific props required to execute a skit are visual aids that can add the dimensions of realism and excitement to your humor. What better way to create humorous images out of words than to act them out with props. Tools and a toolbelt (or sweater and sneakers) can generate an emotional impact on your audience that could not be produced with words. For any humorous skit that you develop, incorporate simple, appropriate, and visually strong props, such as a gorilla, refrigerator, or automatic transmission, that aid but not distract from your delivery. Remember you are the primary audiovisual in the skit, and too many props can steal your thunder and the audience's focus.

Make Eye Contact

Making eye contact with individual students throughout your class when you deliver your humor may be the most important recommendation in this chapter, which probably isn't saying anything you haven't already concluded. (But wait for the next chapter. It gets worse.) Hoff (1992) refers to it as "the electric current that keeps audiences turned on" (p. 155). If you turn off the current for more than a few seconds, you may disconnect their involvement, interest, attention, and brain waves. Eye contact is unique to live presentations, so take advantage of it. The latest technologies in electronic presentations, such as closed circuit television, teleconferencing, electronic character generation, prepackaged electronic courses, the Outernet, and Ren and Stimpy, do not permit eye contact.

As you begin a joke, anecdote, or skit, make eye contact with a student anywhere in the room for a few seconds, long enough to get a sense of acknowledgement, such as a smile. This contact creates a linkage or connection that is a highly personal exchange that says: "I'm talking to you and I'll be back, but don't hold your breath because I have more important things to do, such as walk my dog and cut my toenails." Once this happens, move on to the next student, and the next, in response to their facial expressions reacting to your eyes. As this happens, your humor becomes very personal to those students. The fact that we can practice this technique almost day in and day out with all of our classes should mean mastery of eye contact in no time. As you develop this skill, concentrate systematically on different students, especially those sitting in the back and corners of the room, as well as those hanging from the recessed lights in the ceiling and perched on the window sill ready to jump. Your eye contact with these outliers can be a life-saving maneuver. This is accomplished easily if you are roaming all over the room while you're talking.

For the forms of humor that require audiovisual aids, eye contact will be more difficult. If you're standing next to an overhead projector to reveal quotations, multiple-choice items, or a top 10 list, try to maintain eye contact as you're reading the material on the transparency. You should be so familiar with the material that looking up at your students to monitor their reactions should be automatic. The problem is that the screen is the focus of their attention, not you. Their eyes will be riveted on the screen as they try to read the joke with you. This type of delivery maintains their attention and participation, but reduces eye contact until the joke is over. When the room is darkened during the use of a slide projector, eye contact is impossible.

Similar limitations occur when you present to large audiences, such as those at Chicago Bulls' games. Individual eye contact like the type described with students in your classroom is impossible. The crowd is too large and far away. However, if you're able to move into the audience, make every effort to establish some eye contact with a few individuals and sections of people in your audience. Your eyes should rove to all areas of the auditorium so that the audience feels you're interested in them. This technique coupled with your body movement can maintain their attention for usually as long as an hour. Even with audiovisual aids, it's tough to hold an audience's attention without the benefit of concentrated individual eye contact.

If you have the opportunity to use the power of eye contact as you deliver your humor, it can have a significant impact on your effectiveness. If you pass it up and never look directly at your students or audience, but instead look around, over, and through them, your success may be diminished. This affliction, referred to as "cocktail party eyes," may help you survive a cocktail party, but it won't increase your potential as a humorist. Without eye contact, your delivery is impersonal and distant. If you don't make a conscientious effort to use it, you might as well just hand out your jokes, lecture notes, transparencies, driver's license, and credit cards.

PRACTICE, PRACTICE, PRACTICE Everything

Professional comedians are constantly rehearsing and testing their material. Developing the perfect timing for each joke, spontaneity of movement, physical expressiveness, and vocal vitality in your delivery requires practice, practice, and more practice. A solid performance of your humorous material depends on all of the elements recommended in the preceding pages working together to maximize its laughter potential. If any one of those elements, such as timing or eye contact, is not practiced sufficiently to assure a polished delivery, then the entire performance can unravel or even collapse into what is a.k.a. the "b_ _ _" word, blob.

After you have rehearsed your material by yourself in front of a mirror and straightened your tie or dress (or both if you're Mrs. Doubtfire), continue to practice the material at every opportunity. Since you will seldom be able to set aside ample blocks of time just for practice, consider integrating your rehearsal into time slots already reserved for no-brainer activities, such as relaxing in bed, traveling by car or airplane, mowing the lawn, shoveling snow, bungy jumping, hitch hiking, or neurosurgery. You could also practice during your exercise periods for walking, running, swimming, rock climbing, pole vaulting, dog-sledding, or ski jumping. Some of my best humorous material, in fact, has been created during long runs in my neighborhood while being chased by a pit bull. Maybe it's those endorphins working or being petrified of becoming dog food. I'm not sure.

Once you feel you've reached a comfortable level of delivery, you're ready to begin the field-testing phases described in Chapter 3. First, test your jokes, stories, and other humor formats on secretaries, colleagues, students, friends, and family members, where possible, and escalate the humor discrimination power of these testees during this phase. Second, move to the next level of small social groups, meetings, and your classes. We are extremely fortunate to have readily available captive audiences in our classes to refine our art of teaching and craft of humor. They serve as a "humor bootcamp" to hone your humor skills so that you can BE ALL THAT YOU CAN BE as professors. Since all of your attempts at humor are designed to facilitate learning, your students will continue to benefit as you become more effective at integrating humor into your instruction.

Finally, if you plan to deliver your humor in the context of a keynote address or research presentation to a large audience, be prepared to present only your best material, the tried-and-true winners. Rehearse until your delivery is flawless and then practice some more. You can never be sure how your material will be received by a different audience, especially if they are peers or professionals in another discipline.

Recover from a Bomb Gracefully

Even after following all of the preceding recommendations, you can still bomb on specific punch lines in your "low-risk" humor formats such as multiple-choice items and top 10 lists. Stories can fall flat. Remember these formats are intended to minimize the risk of bombing, not totally eliminate it. What should you do when this happens? There are at least two strategies to consider for successful on-the-spot recovery: (a) keep talking without missing a beat as though nothing had happened and your audience may not realize you bombed, or (b) acknowledge an obvious bomb with a humorous quip, such as "I didn't think it was funny, either," "That's what happens when you test out new material," "My teenage daughter told me it wouldn't work," or "I guess that statement may be true, but it obviously isn't funny." Notice the techniques Leno and Letterman use every night to recover from jokes that bomb. Although the first method is the easiest to execute, the second method can break the tension in the audience because they may feel embarrassed or sorry for you. It's as awkward for them as it is for you, although you will always feel much worse. The follow-up quip helps relieve your sense of humiliation by letting you off the hook and, simultaneously, releases the tension in the audience. If none of those techniques seem to work, you might consider quickly moving to another continent, such as Jupiter.

There are also six reactions to a bomb that you shouldn't exhibit: (a) don't try to explain the joke; it doesn't help plus it can insult your audience, (b) don't whine, gripe, or complain; suffer silently if you need to, (c) don't let it throw you off track; stay focused on the presentation you prepared, (d) don't give up or throw in the towel; the performance must go on, (e) don't blame the audience; they're always right, and (f) don't fake a grand mal seizure to win the audience's sympathy; they'll see right through you.

Critique Your Delivery

If it is possible to videotape or, at minimum, cassette tape your class and professional presentations, you will have a great opportunity to scrutinize every movement you made. Using the recommendations in this chapter as a checklist, analyze your effectiveness quotient on each element in your delivery to diagnose what worked, what bombed, and why. Was it the material or your delivery that was flawed? Make adjustments, revisions, and modifications to every element that needs improvement as soon as possible while the performance is fresh. Then test out those changes in your next class or presentation. You will discover this to be an unending process. However, consider the alternative form of your presentation before you started using humor. Despite the constant challenge to prepare funny material and to deliver it perfectly, you will probably agree that teaching and presenting have never been so much fun.

Chapter 6

Using Humor in the Classroom

The 1997 report by UCLA's Higher Education Research Institute (1997) indicated in a national survey of more than 250,000 freshman at nearly 500 universities that a 30-year record high 35.6% of the students said that they were frequently bored in class. One of the greatest challenges in college teaching is to tackle course content that students perceive as super-boring, ultra-difficult, or anxiety-producing. Probably most students possess one or more of those perceptions about the courses we teach. My students tend to view statistics as a "triple-threat" course. Consequently, I'm in the hole from the get-go. If you combine those student perceptions with a professor who has the charisma of spackling and makes a minimal effort to alter those perceptions, you can really kill the students' learning spirit. I am ashamed to admit that for several years most of the students enrolled in my classes could be distinguished physically by the open gashes, bruises, burns, and dents in their foreheads from passing out face-forward onto their pencils, notebooks, scalding coffee, laptops, and revolvers during my unbearable lectures. Fortunately now, due to my use of humor and breakthroughs in cosmetic surgery, you would hardly be able to detect the scars. It is physically impossible to laugh and snore at the same time. Humor involves active learning.

Effective teaching requires imagination and creativity to turn the students' negative perceptions around. Imagine using humor as a teaching tool for that purpose. The research evidence reviewed previously suggests humor is a potentially powerful strategy for achieving that goal and more. (*Note:* I don't remember if I said this in Chapter 1 and I'm too lazy to go back and check.) So why has humor become a secret weapon that few professors fire from their arsenal of instructional methods? There are at least three possible explanations. First, professors are not trained to use humor in their classrooms. It's not part of any curriculum. There are no training courses or available guidelines to prepare professors to write humorous material, apply it appropriately to their disciplines, and deliver it effectively. Second, related to the lack of training is the perception by many professors that to use humor you have to possess the skills of a professional comedian. After all, you have to be able to tell jokes and anecdotes and to respond to students' questions with witty remarks. Certainly not everyone is capable of doing that successfully. Third, it is believed that professors are not supposed to be stand-up comics or entertainers. Teaching is serious business and humor is frivolous and not dignified. In fact, it is viewed as demeaning to the profession.

What's wrong with this picture? Hopefully, after reading the preceding chapters, you can conclude that the first reason is the primary purpose for writing this book and the other two excuses are misconceptions about the meaning of humor and its instructional usefulness. The notion that you have to have the comedic gifts of Sinbad, Ellen DeGeneres, or Sam Donaldson should be dispelled by now. Any professor can learn to employ both high-risk and low-risk techniques systematically as teaching tools to facilitate learning in their classrooms. The forms of humor presented previously (see Chapter 3) plus those that have been custom tailored for college classroom applications (described in this chapter) provide a completely filled toolbelt with a variety of manual and power tools from which you can select those that fit your humor style, discipline, and students. Finally, the perception of humor as just telling jokes for entertainment value is extremely narrow. Even Robin Williams' teaching role in the *Dead Poets Society* demonstrated how humor is linked to creativity. Humor is a mechanism for creative expression that focuses on "how" we teach, not "what" we teach. Excellence in the "how" requires creativity. As Goodman (1995) has observed, "Humor and creativity are intimately related — there is a connection between HA HA! and AHA!" (p. 41.). Humor is a legitimate strategy for teaching when it is planned properly and used appropriately in the context of the teaching-learning paradigm.

The title of this book suggests that professors and students are from two different planets or candy bars. There are at least a spillion differences between us and them, give or take one or two. Those differences create barriers to our communications that must be broken down if we are to be effective teachers. One of the barriers is the way we think. As professors, it is natural to view "what" we do in the classroom from our personal angle. After all, we are in control and we know "what" needs to be taught. Unfortunately, that is not always the best perspective to determine "how" it should be taught. When we use humor, we should adopt a perspective of empathy for our students. That perspective underlies the development of the techniques suggested in this chapter as well as those in preceding chapters.

The most recent teaching tools involving computer technology, active learning, cooperative and collaborative learning, and critical thinking can be executed without any meaningful connection between professor and students. The techniques require interaction among students in a variety of small group structures and interaction with multimedia software. Despite the mounting empirical evidence on the effectiveness of these techniques in improving learning, the professor can facilitate, direct, and choreograph a vast array of activities at a distance. No professor-student connection is required. Humor can enhance these techniques by breaking down the natural barriers that exist by virtue of our position, title, age, height, and cholesterol level compared with that of our students. The uniqueness of our presence in the classroom (versus a piece of machinery) is a function of our relationships with our students. Humor is one vehicle to make those relationships closer. Considering all of the teaching tools currently in use, what if we could extract the unique contribution of each tool to improve learning. Wouldn't that provide a powerful instructional package for our students.

Think back to your own experience as an undergraduate and graduate student. Now there's a depressing thought. Your serotonin level just took a nosedive. I'm going to pause here for a few minutes while you run and get some Prozac, Nicnac, or Tictac, or carbo-load on a giant bag of M&Ms. Do you feel better now? Are you ready to resume our excursion over the speed bumps of memory lane? Okay, back to the subject of this paragraph, instructional applications of anti-depressants. What traits or behaviors of your professors did you like and dislike? Imagine an eclectic professor who possesses all of the characteristics you admired, respected, and valued as a student. The operative word here is "student." View the strategies for using humor and other teaching tools through your students' eye sockets. Put yourself in their uncomfortable seats. How would they react to what you present? How would humor change the way they respond to the syllabus and other handouts, the examples you use in class, the problems you assign, the reviews you conduct before exams, and the exams themselves? If these effects on the students are positive, and, in some way, facilitate their learning, then you're on the right track.

An impact study of 10 specific strategies for using humor in the classroom which are described in the remainder of this chapter was executed over a three-year period (1994-1996) with three undergraduate and five graduate statistics courses (Berk, 1997a; Berk & Nanda, 1997). The students in all classes rated every humor strategy as "Very Effective" or "Extremely Effective" in reducing their anxiety, improving their ability to learn, and performing their best on problems and exams. In addition, the composite effect of all of the strategies measured with several scales indicated both statistically and practically significant decreases in anxiety and improvements in attitudes toward the course. While these outcomes can not be generalized beyond the statistics courses involved in the study (although I am tempted to go hog wild with my generalizations and you can't restrain me), they contribute preliminary evidence that the effort to systematically incorporate humor into my teaching is worth continuing.

In addition to the piles of evidence from my classes, I've received testimonials by professors who have actually tested these techniques in their own classes:

"Before I tried Ron's humor methods in my philosophy course I had a class attendance problem. Now, no one comes to class."
                    H. I., Slot Machine University, Nevada

"I had never considered humor as a teaching tool. Applying humor to my engineering courses led me to understand the true meaning of humiliation and rejection."
                    J. K., Toyota College, Kentucky

"I took Ron's suggestion about office hours on my economics syllabus and I haven't had to meet with a student since."
                    L. M. N., Hush Puppy Community College, Mississippi

"I used the humor strategies in my gross anatomy course this semester. The cadavers were more responsive than the students."
                    O. P. Q., Oil Slick College of Medicine, Alaska

"My students constantly bombard me with questions after class. Once I started using humor, they didn't hassle me anymore. Instead, I received anonymous Post-its on my office door, such as: 'You are raw industrial sewage.' 'You are a big disgusting bag of cellulite.' 'You should be methodically dismembered and your eyeballs eaten by rats.'"
                    R. S. T. U., Crabcake Community College, Maryland

These authentic experiences certainly speak for themselves. What more compelling evidence could I provide? I bet you're getting really excited to see these amazing techniques. Okay, it's time to reveal them.

From the beginning of class one through the final exam in the last class of each course, there are 10 systematic techniques you can use to integrate humor at every instructional and testing opportunity (Berk, 1997b): (1) humorous material on syllabus, (2) descriptors, cautions, and warnings on handouts, (3) opening jokes, (4) skits/dramatizations, (5) spontaneous humor, (6) humorous questions, (7) humorous examples, (8) humorous problem sets, (9) *Jeopardy!* type reviews for exams, and (10) humorous material on exams. Descriptions with examples of these strategies are presented next.

1. Humorous Material on Syllabus

Usually before anything is said in the first class of the semester, students receive the syllabus, which is irrefutably the most boring handout on earth. It is their first glimpse into what the course will cover and first impression of the character of the professor. In other words, the syllabus can be one of several tone-setters for determining what the class will be like for the next 15 weeks. Anxiety in the students' minds as they enter any undergraduate or graduate course can be extremely high. In my subject area, math anxiety and other negative baggage about the horror stories students tell about statistics courses tend to contribute to negative attitudes toward the content before any professor has uttered his or her first word.

In an attempt to communicate "this course is not going to be as bad or difficult or boring as you think," humorous material can be inserted into six elements of the syllabus: (1) title, (2) prerequisites, (3) professor's credentials, (4) office hours, (5) teaching strategies, and (6) reading list.

Title. What appears on the first page typically has the strongest impact. For example, under the course title of any syllabus, you can place a descriptor commonly used on food and household products, such as "NEW AND IMPROVED," "MICROWAVE SAFE," or "FAT FREE/CHOLESTEROL FREE." The incongruity is a natural. Students do not expect to see anything unusual on a formal, predictably boring syllabus. The unexpected twist of a food label on the expected course title creates a humorous situation. In fact, the label can be used on any class handout, even exams. Below is a list of other descriptors I have compiled for use on syllabi and handouts for a variety of courses:

ENVIRONMENTALLY SAFE	NOT FROM CONCENTRATE
BIODEGRADABLE	100% FLORIDA SQUEEZED
PHOSPHATE FREE	KOSHER QUALITY
DISHWASHER SAFE	WEATHER RESISTANT
INDUSTRIAL STRENGTH	REGULAR or EXTRA LIGHT
MAXIMUM STRENGTH	ULTRA LIGHT or ULTRA FAT FREE

RECYCLABLE	NATURALLY FAT FREE/ARTIFICIAL FLAVORS
SODIUM FREE	INDIVIDUALLY WRAPPED
LOW CALORIE	LOCALLY PRODUCED
SUGAR FREE	REFRIGERATE AFTER OPENING
DOLPHIN SAFE	NO ARTIFICIAL PRESERVATIVES
CAFFEINE FREE	SWEETENED WITH NUTRASWEET
NO ARTIFICIAL COLORS	NATURALLY DECAFFEINATED
BAKED WITH PRIDE	PROVIDES 12 VITAMINS AND MINERALS
MICROWAVABLE	AVAILABLE IN ASSORTED FLAVORS
NATURAL LEMON FLAVOR	GOURMET SUPER QUALITY
QUICKSTARTING	SUPER CHUNKY, THICK AND SPICY

A THIRD LESS CONTENT, SAME GREAT TASTE!

Prerequisites. On the first class as students are seriously examining the syllabus, another element they do not expect to see is humorous prerequisites. This also is presented on the first page for maximum impact. The twist of jocular prerequisites usually elicits mirthful responses because the students simply can't believe what they're reading. If there are no real prerequisites, use the humorous ones; if there are real ones, list those first and then add the humorous ones. This is the old humor formula of presenting the expected, followed by the unexpected twist. For example, in my undergraduate introductory statistics course with no prerequisites, I display the following:

PREREQUISITES: One semester of *Sesame Street, Mister Rogers, Barney,* or the equivalent.

The graduate course has real and imaginary prerequisites presented as follows:

PREREQUISITES: Undergraduate statistics NR100.308, two semesters of *Sesame Street, Home Improvement,* or *The X-Files,* or the equivalent.

Professor's Credentials. Another humorous technique is to make mock of your own degrees, licenses, and rank which typically appear somewhere near the top of the first page of the syllabus. It provides a key opportunity to convey a first impression of what you are going to be like. If you don't take yourself super-seriously, joking about your credentials is one mechanism to demonstrate that.

In the healthcare field, most everyone in medicine and nursing have lots of letters after their degrees to signify different licenses and certifications. Since I work in that field but have no real letters, I use the letters as a vehicle for my humor. For example:

Ronald A. Berk, PhD, CNN, ESPN, CSPAN, and All-Around Fun Guy.

Many undergraduate and graduate students who are entering one of my statistics classes for the first time have anxiety levels through the ceiling. Those additions after my degree can relieve fear-of-the-professor syndrome lickety split. I have just knocked myself off any professorial pedestal. In fact, I try to place myself under the pedestal.

If one of our primary goals in using humor as a teaching tool is to break down barriers to communication and learning, self-effacing humor can be very effective in the attainment of that goal. Formal titles and degrees can be intimidating to students. Requiring them to call you Dr. ... or professor ... erects a gigantic barrier and establishes an enormous distance between you and them. Breaking down these walls so that students perceive you as human and, more importantly, approachable can facilitate learning. Students will be less hesitant and inhibited about asking questions in and out of class and approaching you to talk about problems they may be having with some topic and their need for help.

A way of reinforcing the image you created on the syllabus is to introduce yourself with the same tone to "officially" break down the communication barriers. I begin with the following remarks:

> I'm Ron Berk and I'd like to welcome you to (name) course. Please call me Ron. You've all read my titles and there is nothing that I have done that you can't do. The basic difference between us is that I stayed in school longer. Right now, you may have respect for my position of professor, but Ron has to earn your respect. I want to make every effort to work WITH you as a team, not above you, to move you as far as you can go to attain the objectives of this course. You will learn more about (subject) than you can possibly imagine, probably more than you want to learn, and we are going to have fun doing it. By the way, to those of you obsessive-compulsives or anal-retentives who have checked me out in advance, I can say that everything you've heard about this course and me is probably true.

What is the impact of this opening statement on class one of the semester? My undergraduates (juniors) exhibit the basic clinical symptoms of shock. They turn blue, mouths drop open, eyeballs bulge out of their sockets, and probably the one thought of disbelief racing through their brains is: "Is he for real?" My comments certainly break the tension at the beginning of the class and drop their anxiety levels a few notches. This dramatic effect on the juniors may be attributable to the humongous gap between our ages and academic positions coupled with the basic humor formula of juxtaposing the expected with the unexpected. Their conditioned expectations of the course and me explode before their bulging eyes. The sudden unexpected twist in what I say doesn't produce humor, but it surely blows several students off their beach chairs.

The masters and doctoral students, on the other hand, exhibit less evidence of trauma, most likely because they are much older and more mature than the undergraduates and have full-time jobs and families. In general, they are light blue, mouths are only half-way open, eyeballs are still in their sockets, and they are more serious, inhibited, and emotionally restrained. They typically show fewer outward signs of emotion in reacting to anything in the course. In other words, when it comes to humor, graduate students can be a tough audience. Many of these characteristics may be due to the greater complexity of their lives. While I'm talking, they may be thinking:

- "I've got to get home to my sick kid."
- "Why did I eat those burritos and beans for lunch?"
- "How can I get my windshield wipers to work to drive home through that 25-mile carwash?"
- "What should I make for dinner tonight?"
- "When I get home, I really don't want to clean that meat-eating algae slime on the bottom of the refrigerator."
- "I need to call the exterminator to get rid of those giant crickets lurking out side our front door that devour UPS drivers who can't drop and run fast enough."

That's pretty stiff competition for gaining and maintaining their undivided attention for what I have to say.

I suspect some of you are probably concerned about how the jocular credentials and introductory remarks affect the students' respect for me. It is my feeling that the students possess and demonstrate a greater sense of respect for me as a person and as a professor. The most visible signs that support this feeling are: (a) most students will still address me as "Dr." for the rest of the semester, and (b) many will approach me after class or in my office to discuss personal problems as well as course-related matters. By self-effacing my credentials, I convey confidence and security with myself that increase not decrease my credibility. The students are probably thinking: "Since he asked us to call him Ron, he's okay. Anyone that can say that deserves to be addressed by their title." There are few undergraduate and many graduate students who always address me as Ron. Regardless of what the students call me, there is personal satisfaction that I have succeeded in breaking down a major barrier that will hopefully facilitate the learning process by relaxing and opening their minds to receive my messages and directions.

Office Hours. Since students need to know when you are available, your office hours furnish another opportunity for the unexpected. Identify hours that would be impossible or unreasonable for full-time students and faculty to meet, such as:

MWF 4:30 AM – 7:00 AM

TTH 9:00 PM – 12:00 AM

Open all legal and illegal holidays

Closed Sunday for mental repairs

For part-time evening students who work full-time, present morning and afternoon hours at which they couldn't possibly be available, such as:

MWF 10:12 AM – 3:24 PM

TTH 1:07 AM – 4:53 AM

When you review the syllabus in class, it would be helpful to present the "real" hours, if you have any.

Teaching Strategies. The fifth place on the syllabus where humor can be inserted is in the list of teaching strategies. The three methods most frequently mentioned are lecture, discussion, and small groups. Rather traditional, wouldn't you say? A list containing the expected strategies followed by absolutely ridiculous, outrageous, and inappropriate methods in your subject and class structure creates the incongruity needed for the humor. In my statistics courses, I present the following:

Lecture, small groups, dramatic presentation, peer critique and humiliation, stand-up comedy, IMAX movies, field trips, hand-to-hand combat, picnics, and cruises.

The students' initial impression after reading this on the syllabus is: "This course is going to be fun!" However, they still keep asking, "When's the cruise?" Simply adding those few unexpected methods can contribute toward building positive attitudes toward the course.

Reading List. The recommended reading list, bibliography, or references attached to the syllabus furnishes another opportunity for humor. Humorous references that poke fun at the topics in your course and professional publications should be mixed in with the "real" references, which usually means alphabetized by author. A few examples of humorous statistical references are shown below:

Eses, S. P. (1989). Multivariate log-linear regression factorial analysis of covariance. *Annals of Boredom, 67,* 1190–1260.

Gray, J. (1996). *MANOVA is from Mars, WOMANOVA is from Venus.* Uranus: Misunderstood Multivariate Publishers.

Lipton, T. J. (1992, 4 PM). Differential effects of caffeinated versus decaffeinated t-tests. *British Journal of Statistical Beverages, 29,* 463–470.

Meany, U. R. A. (1995). Regression toward the spleen effect: Clinical manifestations of mediocrity. In N. O. Median & Q. Modo (Eds.), *Mediocrity means never having to reach significance!* (pp. 243-269). Lake Wobegon: Central Tendency Press.

Mulder, F. W., & Scully, D. K. (1996). Alien or outlier? Weird Characteristics of paranormal distributions. In C. Carter (Ed.), *Tales from the $\overline{X}$-files* (Vol. 1, pp. 118-137). Hollywood: The-Truth-Is-Out-There Publishing.

Scared, I. M. (1994). Statisticophobia: Reducing anxiety to p < .05. *Standard Deviates Quarterly, 14,* 47–58.

Compared to the preceding five humorous entries in the syllabus, the effectiveness of the above references in reducing anxiety and improving attitudes is less significant and delayed. That is not necessarily because the references may not be funny. The problem is that few students may even glance at those references in an introductory course. In intermediate and advanced courses where students are forced to consult references when they apply statistics to their thesis or other research projects, there is a better chance that the humor will be noticed. The issue seems to be exposure. The students have to use the references to appreciate them and there is no way to predict that event unless a specific assignment is given. Consequently, the benefits to be gained from humorous references may be greater in graduate than in undergraduate courses.

In addition to all of the foregoing techniques for integrating humor into your syllabus, there are probably many others you can think of or are presently using. Certainly it wouldn't be difficult to exaggerate or embellish the information in other sections of the syllabus, such as a line added to the course description in statistics that says: This course is specifically designed for the "mathematically arthritic" and "computer illiterate." The course objectives, schedule, assignments, and requirements also have jocular potential for the twisted mind. One caution, however, needs to be heeded: Don't overdo it. In our zeal to incorporate humor, we can get carried away by crossing the line between facilitating and distracting and by losing sight of how the powerful tool of humor should be applied correctly. "Hey, let's be careful out there!"

2. Descriptors, Cautions, and Warnings on Handouts

The numerous handouts we distribute in our classes can take a variety of forms. The content may be descriptive information, a research article, examples, practice exercises, or homework assignments.

"Handouts" may even be prepackaged and sold in the bookstore at the beginning of the semester or distributed in small doses throughout the semester. They may be thick or thin and reproduced on blinding neon colored paper to keep students awake or dull white. Despite all of these variations in their physical appearance and substance, usually every handout has a cover page with a title of some kind. That's the only requirement for inserting humor into any handout.

The serious, albeit boring, cover page can be altered in two ways: (1) place a humorous descriptor or label under the title, and (2) list several cautions or warnings about the content contained in the handout. The incongruity for the humor on the cover is generated using the same strategy applied to the syllabus — adding an unexpected element to an expected serious document. It consists of selecting well-known, common descriptors or labels, cautions, and warnings found on food, household products, medicines and drug prescriptions, and road signs and using them totally out of context where you would never expect to see them. This approach was illustrated previously by placing descriptors such as "DISHWASHER SAFE" under the title of the syllabus. Those same descriptors can be added to the title on the cover page of any handout.

The second strategy is choose three or four cautions, warnings, or information labels and list them under the appropriate heading on the bottom half of the cover. Since that space is usually empty, the labels can provide a filler with comic relief to boot. Examples of cautions and warnings as they would appear on a cover are shown below:

CAUTIONS:
- DO NOT operate a motor vehicle or dangerous machinery while reading this material.
- If DROWSINESS occurs, it shouldn't be surprising.
- DO NOT induce vomiting, the content will take care of that.
- DO NOT remove this protective cover under penalty of law.

    or

WARNINGS:
- DO NOT read near fire or flame.
- Avoid ingestion, inhalation, or prolonged contact with skin.
- The possibility of electrical shock does exist if you remove this cover.

An extensive list of sample cautions, warnings, and information labels or notices from which you can pick any for different handout covers is given below:

CAUTIONS:

- Close cover before striking.
- May cause drowsiness.
- Use care when operating a car or dangerous machinery.
- Keep away from sunlight.
- Keep away from pets.
- If a rash, irritation, redness, or swelling develops, discontinue use.
- Tumble dry only.
- Avoid extreme temperatures.
- Store in cool, dry place.
- Hard hat and safety goggles are required.
- Recommended for adults over 21
- Keep away from moisture, rain, snow, sleet, gloom of night, and so forth.
- DO NOT fold, mutilate, or spindle.
- To avoid accidental _____, remove appropriate tab or cover write- protect notch with tape.
- DO NOT leave unattended.
- Watch for fallen rocks.

WARNINGS:

- Keep away from children.
- Substantial penalty for early withdrawal.
- DO NOT puncture, incinerate, or store above 300° F.
- Package not child-resistant.
- DO NOT drink alcoholic beverages when reading this paper.
- Avoid excessive heat above 175° C.
- Keep out of reach from children. In case of accidental overdose (exposure), seek professional assistance immediately.
- DO NOT use near fire or flame.
- May be harmful if swallowed.
- Fatal if taken internally.
- This text may contain explicit material some readers may find objectionable; professional guidance is advised.
- This paper is intended for the private use of our readers and any reproduction, rebroadcast, or any other accounts of this content without the prior written consent of _____ is strictly prohibited.

- DO NOT exceed recommended dosage.
- DO NOT place near a magnetic source.
- DO NOT use if safety seal is broken.
- The Surgeon General of the U.S. has warned that reading this paper could be hazardous to your health and the best safeguard is abstinence.
- This warning label may self-destruct or burn if placed in an environment capable of combustion.
- If this document should ignite, place in a nonflammable container.
- If this document should ignite, do not inhale fumes or permit smoke to get in your eyes nor should you touch the material at any time.
- "Lovely to look at, delightful to hold; but if you break it, consider it sold."

INFORMATION:

- A battery is not needed for operation of this _____.
- The characters in this work are imaginary.
- All sales are final.
- Allow 4–6 weeks for delivery.
- A paid political announcement.
- No purchase necessary; you need not be present to win.
- Objects in mirror are closer than they appear.
- Unleaded gasoline only.
- Member F.D.I.C.
- Discard after use.
- For topical use only.
- See crimp for lot no. and expiration date.
- Filled by weight not volume.
- For external use only.
- Consult your physician if symptoms persist for more than 7 days.
- Action figures sold separately.
- Sold for industrial use only.
- Batteries not included.
- If any defects are discovered, do not attempt to fix them yourself; return to an authorized service center.
- Quantities are limited while supplies last.

- Hardware and instructions are included and wattages stated are maximum recommended.
- Tested and rated by Underwriter's Laboratories.
- Color monitor not included.

3. Opening Jokes

As noted previously, the opening tone you set for the first class of the semester as well as every other one that follows primes your students for what they can expect from you. You control the class atmosphere and, to some extent, the students' levels of stress and anxiety and attitude toward the course. The positive or negative direction of all of this affect can markedly influence their performance in the course. If the humor is intended to produce positive affect and increase achievement, then we need to plan systematically how it can be employed to attain those objectives.

There are three specific purposes for opening class with humorous material: (1) to motivate students to be on time or else they'll miss the joke (it provides a reason to look forward to going to my class rather than to dread or avoid it like the bubonic plague); (2) to serve as a release valve for the stress, tension, anxiety, and negative baggage they bring into class (once they're laughed, maybe their minds will be free and open to receive what I have to present); and (3) to trigger a "fun" attitude toward what's coming up next (Hellooo! Isn't learning supposed to be fun?), since it is fair to assume that much of the content we may teach is super-boring, required to graduate, and unrelated to what is really important in life.

On the first class, once the syllabus and other handouts laced with jocular insertions have been reviewed, you have the option of enforcing the students' mirthful reactions to those documents by beginning the class with a joke to communicate "we are going to have fun this semester" or extinguishing their reactions by jumping right into serious business. I'll give you a wild guess as to my decision choice.

A wide range of forms of humorous material can be used at the opening of every class. Virtually every method described in Chapter 3 can be applied here, including: (a) stand-up jokes, (b) quotations and questions, (c) cartoons, (d) multiple-choice items, (e) top 10 lists, and (f) anecdotes. Plus, there are a few other formats that can be employed.

One preliminary issue in selecting the humor is its relationship to the message of your lecture. The linkage of the point of the humor to the content of your presentation is desirable but not essential (Bryant et al., 1980a; Zillmann & Bryant, 1983). In view of the aforementioned purposes of opening humor, the linkage is more of a luxury than a necessity. Certainly there are some jokes, anecdotes, quotations, and even multiple-choice items and top 10 lists that can be chosen or written for a specific topic. However, if you teach 30 classes per course and there are two to four courses per semester, we're talking about a kagillion jokes. If you can't determine a linkage between every piece of humor and the content, it's okay. Don't stretch it or force a linkage that isn't there. The students will see right through you.

In addition to the humor formats previously suggested, there are a few other one-shot humorous handouts that can simply be distributed at the beginning of class. The students can read the handout while they're waiting for class to start. This gives them an opportunity for a few giggles, maybe a chuckle, or even a cackle or guffaw before you say anything. Talk about low-risk humor in the classroom; that's about as low as you can get.

A variety of generic and professional humor materials for these handouts can be prepared, such as diets, medications, stories, letters, articles, memos, cartoons, pictures, and even joke quizzes. Excellent sources for these different formats are Abrahams (1993), Ellenbogen (1989), Scherr (1983), Waldoks (1994), and Warlock (1990, 1995). These along with others are listed in Chapter 4. Here are a few ideas for one-shot handouts:

Berk's No Stress Diet
(Place on Refrigerator After Opening)

BREAKFAST
1/2 Grapefruit

1 slice whole wheat toast

8 oz. skim milk

LUNCH
4 oz. broiled chicken breast without skin

1 cup steamed zucchini

1 Oreo cookie

Herb tea

MID-AFTERNOON SNACK
Rest of the package of Oreos

1 quart Rocky Road ice cream

1 jar hot fudge

DINNER
Double Quarter Pounder with cheese

Super large fries

Jumbo soda

Bag of Snickers miniatures

1 Dove ice cream bar

Entire frozen cheesecake eaten directly
from the freezer

MIDNIGHT SNACK

Large Dominos pepperoni & mushroom pizza

(*Note:* The above diet can be presented in conjunction with the "Top 10 Diet Tips" listed in Chapter 3. If they can be scheduled right before midterms or final exams or Thanksgiving or Christmas, the students will really appreciate it. In fact, many of my students have found this diet with tips to be the most useful handout of the semester. They actually post it on their refrigerators.)

I'm Tired

Yes, I'm tired. For several years I've been blaming it on middle-age, iron poor blood, lack of vitamins, air pollution, water pollution, nutrasweet, obesity, dieting, underarm odor, yellow wax build-up, and a dozen other maladies that make you wonder if life is really worth living.

But now I find out, it ain't that.

I'm tired because I am overworked.

The population of this country is 200 million. Eighty-four million are retired. That leaves 116 million to do the work. There are 75 million in school, which leaves 41 million to do the work. Of this total, there are 22 million employed by the federal government.

That leaves 19 million to do the work. Four million are in the armed forces, which leaves 15 million to do the work. Take from that total the 14,800,000 people who work for the state and city governments and that leaves 200,000 to do the work. There are 188,000 in hospitals, so that leaves 12,000 to do the work. Now, there are 11,998 people in prisons. That leaves just 2 people to do the work. You and me. And you're sitting here reading this. No wonder I'm tired.

Self-Esteem

Everyone knows that having positive self-esteem is good. So, of course, having poor self-esteem leads naturally to a miserable life. This is obvious. What I would like to point out is that good self-esteem is bad for the economy! Think about it . . . If everyone had good self-esteem, the first thing that would happen is that all the psychiatrists would be out-of-business. Then all the advertising people would be out of a job, because consumers would no longer fall for the advertising gimmick of trying to convince us that we would be sexier/more attractive/healthier/happier if we bought yet one more stupid product. Then, of course, most of the lawyers would go belly-up, because people with self-esteem don't have a need to sue one another at the drop of a hat. Most of the auto industry would fold-up because people with self-esteem don't need three cars or fancy cars to impress their neighbors. Anyway, I think you can see the domino effect here. If all Americans had good self-esteem, our economy would fall apart, leaving us wide-open to an economic assault by our international competitors. Oh, sure, we'd have strong self-esteem, but "Made In America" would be a thing of the past. Do you want this to happen?? (Magadatz, 1993, p. 26)

A Letter from a Mom to Her Son

Dear Son,

I'm writing this slow cause you can't read fast. We don't live where we did when you left. Your dad read in the paper where the most accidents happened within twenty miles of home, so we moved. I won't be able to send you the address cause the last family that lived here took the numbers with them for their next house so they wouldn't have to change their address.

This place has a washing machine. The first day I put four shirts in it, pulled the chain and haven't seen 'em since. It only rained twice this week, three days the first time, and four days the second time. The coat you wanted me to send you, your Aunt Sue said it would be a little too heavy to send in the mail, with the heavy buttons, so we cut them off and put them in the pockets.

We got a bill from the funeral home ... said if we didn't make the last payment on Grandma's funeral bill, up she comes.

Your father has a lovely job. He now has over 500 men under him. He's cutting grass at the cemetery.

Your sister had a baby this morning. I haven't found out whether it's a boy or girl, so I don't know if you're an aunt or an uncle.

Your Uncle John fell in the whiskey vat. Some men tried to pull him out but he fought them off playfully, so he drowned. Took the mortician four hours to wipe that silly grin off his face. We had him cremated. He burned for three days. Three of your friends went off the bridge in a pickup truck. One was driving, the other two were in the back. The driver got out by rolling down the window and he swam to safety. The other two drowned; they just couldn't get the tailgate down.

Not much more news this time. Nothing much has happened.

With lots of love,

Mom

P.S. I'm sorry. I was going to send you some money but the envelope was already sealed.

(Adapted from Warlock, 1995, p. 285).

Berk's Political Astuteness Quiz: Part Uno*

DIRECTIONS: Match the WORDS in Column I with the appropriate "Politically-Correct" TERMS in Column II. Write the letter of your answer choice in the blank to the left of each number. You may use the choices in Column II once or not at all.

Column I	Column II
__ 1. Alive	A. Chemically Inconvenienced
__ 2. Dead	B. Sexually Dysfunctional
__ 3. Stoned	C. Cerebrally Challenged
__ 4. Dishonest	D. Involuntarily Leisured
__ 5. Lazy	E. Increasingly Distracted
__ 6. Bald	F. Cosmetically Different
__ 7. Fired	G. Living Impaired
__ 8. Ugly	H. Chronologically Gifted
__ 9. Old	I. Metabolically Abled
__10. Stupid	J. Follicularly Challenged
	K. Motivationally Deficient
	L. Parasitically Oppressed
	M. Ethically Disoriented

*Terms taken from Beard and Cerf (1994).

Berk's Political Astuteness Quiz: Part Dos*

DIRECTIONS: Match the WORDS in Column I with the appropriate "Politically-Correct" TERMS in Column II. Write the letter of your answer choice in the blank to the left of each number. You may use the choices in Column II once or not at all.

Column I	Column II
__ 1. Airhead	A. Uniquely Coordinated
__ 2. Book	B. Insignificant Other
__ 3. Robot	C. Incompletely Successful
__ 4. Prostitute	D. Optically Inconvenienced
__ 5. Ex-Spouse	E. Processed Tree Carcass
__ 6. Farsighted	F. Uniquely Proficient
__ 7. Late	G. Indefinitely Idled
__ 8. Boring	H. Charm-Free
__ 9. Incompetent	I. Socially Misaligned
__ 10. Unemployed	J. Sex Care Provider
	K. Cerebro-Atmospheric Person
	L. Temporally Challenged
	M. Mechanical-American

*Terms taken from Beard and Cerf (1994)

DATASET®
(STATIUM)

The most widely prescribed medication for reducing anxiety in statistics classes throughout America.

Are you doing everything you can to reduce your anxiety, but it just never seems to be enough?

Tests prove DATASET® helps reduce anxiety when your professor doesn't know how. Of course, not everyone gets the same results. And not everyone on DATASET® reaches their anxiety-reducing goal.

Consider the following case study:

> **Brunhilda has high anxiety and her mother had high anxiety in her statistics class when she was getting her degree.**
> This put Brunhilda at risk. High anxiety is serious, especially if you have 2 or more risk factors, including: taking statistics while working full-time, having a family, or having a humorless, stodgy statistics professor.
>
> **Once she realized the risk, Brunhilda tried really hard to reduce her anxiety.**
> For six months she ignored her family in order to complete her statistics assignments. She met with a study group of other classmates in a yellow cab every Saturday morning. The statistician said that these sacrifices don't always reduce anxiety enough. It could be genes or body chemistry; no one knows for sure.
>
> **The statistician prescribed DATASET®.**
> The statistician added DATASET® to Brunhilda's anxiety-reduction program and her anxiety really started to plummet!

Is DATASET® right for you?

Ask your statistician. DATASET® should not be used by people who are allergic to broccoli, concrete, or maggots, people with hemorrhoids or hernias, or people who are chronically exhausted. Because of possible drug interactions, tell your statistician about any medications you are taking (not that he/she will necessarily do anything about it).

There can be side effects.

It is recommended that your statistician perform routine tests, such as Tea-tests and multiple aggression analysis, before and after treatment. Tell your statistician if you experience any unexplained pains while taking DATASET®, as this could be a sign of serious side effects, such as schizophrenia, sadomasochism, or necrophilia.

DATASET® is available in 500 mg tablets or time-release suppositories.

Ask your statistician about DATASET®.
For a free booklet, call 1-800-STATIUM.

BERK PHARMACEUTICALS
(A name you used to be able to trust!)

MEMOSTOP®
(Memotine Transdermal System)

Recommend MEMOSTOP® 10 mg/day to the memo writers who are making your life miserable. An effective aid to a comprehensive memo-writing cessation program.

- In clinical studies in a few really big name universities, quit rates were significantly higher in the MEMOSTOP® group than in the placebo group.

Designed for 24-hour control of memotine craving and other withdrawal symptoms.

- Therapeutic memotine levels are maintained even early in the morning when the urges seem to be the greatest.

Memotine transdermal dots (MTD) are available in weekly packages of 7. A black dot is placed at the tip of the nose. If this humiliation doesn't decrease memo writing, then the entire 8-week weaning program is recommended. It consists of a convenient "4-2-2" schedule for memotine elimination. This dosage schedule has proven effectiveness even with the most "anal retentive" administrators. Dots shown below are "actual size."

          ●

4 weeks—	2 weeks—	2 weeks—
Initiate and maintain	Step down to	Step down to
MEMOSTOP® 10 mg/day	MEMOSTOP® 6 mg/day	MEMOSTOP® 3 mg/day

MEMOSTOP® Support Services include:

- **The MEMOSTOP® Hotline**: Patients talk one-on-one with advisors who "like" to listen to sordid stories; psychic advice is given as a free bonus.
- **The MEMOSTOP® Compliance Program**: We'll remind patients to take MEMOSTOP® with a daily phone call in pig Latin; we don't trust patients to comply with anything.
- **The MEMOSTOP® Referral Service**: A directory of local memo-writing cessation programs with pictures of members.

These services are free to all MEMOSTOP® patients for a full year.

The SQUAB Commitment to patients: "We don't trust you, but you'll learn to trust us" (or "A bird in the hand can make a mess"). It's difficult to stop writing memos and memo writers may relapse. That's why we've made a commitment to patients who relapse. If a patient decides to try MEMOSTOP® again, we'll provide rebates and continued access to the Support Services.

WARNINGS: Memotine from any source can be toxic and addictive. The risk of memotine replacement in a memo-writing cessation program should be weighed against the hazard of continued memo writing and its effects on employees, and the likelihood of achieving cessation without memotine replacement.

PRECAUTIONS: The patient should be urged to stop memo writing completely when initiating MEMOSTOP® therapy. This may produce adverse effects in the forms of sulking, whining, foot-in-the-mouth disease, or the compulsion to eat crow.

For further information, phone 1-800-MEMODOT.
SQUAB DOT COMPANY
(We make dots for all diseases)

PROPAINE®
with Kosherdil (1%)

The first medication proven effective to remove excess hair in a jiff. Available in an easy-to-use aerosol spray.

If you have unsightly hair on your knuckles, nose (unless you're a witch), elbows, or any other part of your anatomy, **PROPAINE®** can blow it off with just a single spray.

Defuzz unwanted hair so that it will never be seen again. The added ingredient Kosherdil (10 mg per ml of **PROPAINE®**) penetrates to the root of your follicles. Kills follicles REALLY DEAD! Produces instant baldness in the area applied.

- Recommended by 1 out of 10 dermatologists on the run
- #1 choice of orangutans, werewolves, and really hairy people worldwide
- Immediate results in a whole bunch of patients

Contraindications: **PROPAINE®** should not be used by people who are afraid of campfires, cookouts, candle-lighting ceremonies, and severe pain.

Side Effects: No serious reactions other than third-degree burns. Side effects found in a triple- blind clinical study of patients include hemorrhaging, paralysis, vertigo, trichinosis, gangrene, and anthrax.

Precautions: Discontinue **PROPAINE®** if skin disappears or if one major organ after another shuts down. DO NOT use in conjunction with other topical agents such as motor oil, horseradish, or Bearnaise sauce.

UPCHUCK COMPANY
(Pyrotechnics Division)

ARE YOU LONELY?
WORKING ON YOUR OWN?
HATE MAKING DECISIONS?

HOLD A MEETING

YOU CAN...

- MEET PEOPLE
- DRAW PICTURES
- FEEL SIGNIFICANT
- LEARN COMMUNICATION SKILLS
- MAYBE EVEN IMPRESS
  YOUR COLLEAGUES

ALL ON YOUR
INSTITUTION'S
TIME!!!

MEETINGS
(THE PRACTICAL ALTERNATIVE TO WORK!)

HAVE AN

AVERAGE
DAY.

Warlock, A. (1995). *250 Funniest office jokes, memos and cartoon pinups* (Vol. 2). Collinsville, IL: Knightraven Books.

4. Skits/Dramatizations

Among the various forms of humor that are appropriate for a class opening, the skit is one of the most powerful. Although the *Home Improvement* and *Mister Rogers'* skits outlined in Chapter 3 can be applied to a variety of topics in any course, there is another that I developed just for the first class of the semester.

After the handouts are distributed at the beginning and before I introduce myself or say anything to the class, I completely darken the room, which is somewhat scary by itself, pause a few moments to build tension, and then with a miniature flashlight in hand, read the following:

> STATISTICS
>
> The final Frontier.
>
> These are the voyages of *STAT TREK!*
>
> Its 15 week mission:
>   To explore strange new statistics;
>   To seek out new methods for conducting research;
>   To boldly go where no statistician has gone before!

Then I play the theme music from *Star Trek* and flip the overhead projector light on with a blue transparency containing stars and the words:

> *STAT TREK*
>
> Where No Statistician Has Gone Before!

After the music is turned off and room lights turned on, I tell the students "This course will be unlike any class you've had before. We are going to have fun with statistics and this is just the beginning."

Does that three-minute skit set a tone for the first class as well as the whole semester, or what? You could probably devise other versions of this skit around the __?__ TREK theme and extend it to __?__ TREK: The Next Generation for a presentation that proposes a new direction or approach.

Other dramatizations can involve small groups of students. They can be executed (the dramatizations, that is) at any appropriate time during the class to illustrate a concept or a procedure. A visual presentation can be more memorable than just a verbal explanation (I keep repeating this because I forgot what I said in Chapter 5 which was kinda verbal). For example, intermediate statistics topics, such as stepwise multiple regression and analysis of covariance, can be introduced with dramatizations of mathematical processes:

Multiple Regression

Students are selected to serve as predictor and criterion variables. As a pool of six predictor students and one criterion student stand in front of the class, the rest of the class can be asked to identify: (1) the first predictor student with the most characteristics in common (e.g., height, hair color, gender, glasses-no glasses, slacks-dress) (*Note:* Don't even think about using size, weight, or ethnicity) with the criterion student, (2) the second predictor student with one or more additional characteristics in common with the criterion student but having few or no characteristics in common with the first predictor student, and (3) the third predictor student with at least one characteristic not accounted for by the first two predictor students and few or no characteristics in common with them. This stepwise selection process of student variables is visual and conceptual. The concepts of the stepwise inclusion criteria for entry of predictor variables into an equation, unique contribution of each successive predictor, and increments in R^2 or R^2 change are anchored in the dramatization as the correlation matrix is then analyzed. The students then walk through the quantitative process with an unusual set of variables:

Intercorrelation Matrix of Six Predictors and the Criterion

Predictor	2	3	4	5	6	WEASEL
1. Dinky	.17	.77	.93	.26	.42	.63
2. Rinky		.69	.87	.10	.19	.81
3. Binky			.52	.75	.78	.57
4. Tinky				.58	.84	.75
5. Winky					.10	.48
6. Linky						.22

Analysis of Covariance

A four-meter relay race involving four students to the tune of *Rocky* or *Chariots of Fire* is used to demonstrate the concept of posttest means adjusted for initial pretest differences. Based on a pretest-posttest control-group design, two students are chosen to represent pre- and posttests for the treatment sample and two others as the same measures for the control sample. The two pretest students on one side of the room are set to begin the race, but one is given an advantage of a one meter head start to illustrate unequal sample pretest means. Each is given a baton, such as a paper towel roll, lead pipe, or flag pole. When the music begins, the two pretest students run in slow motion across the room to hand off their batons to the two posttest students poised at unequal distances. Once the batons are passed, the posttest students sprint in slow motion toward the finish line. The initial lead by one of the two pretest students is closed as the posttest students cross the finish much closer together. The difference between the original posttest differences and the finish line posttest differences demonstrates the concepts of unadjusted and adjusted posttest means, respectively, and the point where the adjustment occurs based on the pretest or covariate differences. As this slow motion relay race is performed to the music, the students applaud and cheer the runners. This is certainly a new spin on the strategy of active learning. Everyone is involved, mentally and physically.

Any dramatization must be planned meticulously to assure the concept being presented will be exaggerated to improve learning, not detract from it. The roles for the students must be clearly defined and fun, and must never require any task that is embarrassing or difficult to perform; if it is either, the students will refuse to do it or, after class, they'll tie you to a chair with duct tape and force you to watch the movie, *Ace Ventura Snorts Sushi*. Since the entire class participates in these exercises, it can have a strong positive impact on learning, one that the students may never forget.

5. Spontaneous Humor

There can be at least three targets of spontaneous humor in the classroom: (1) the students, (2) yourself, and (3) physical distractions and equipment breakdowns. The first is, by far, the most common form of spontaneous humor simply because it presents more opportunities than the other two forms.

Responses to Students' Questions. "Ad-libs" in response to students questions and comments are the most frequently found type of humor in college classrooms (Bryant et al., 1980a). Its uses and risks were previously examined in the context of high-risk humor (see Chapter 3). However, if the humor can be applied judiciously to avoid the temptations of put-downs and other forms of offensive humor and instead focus on "positive" targets that compliment and uplift the students, witty or clever responses can be very effective. It helps promote an informal, relaxed, nonthreatening, and "fun" classroom environment that is conducive to learning. When an opportunity occurs and you have an appropriate humorous thought, say it. Constant practice in the variety of classroom situations you encounter will improve your humor skills and ability to think humorously.

Responses to Your Mistakes. Another form of spontaneous humor is self-effacing humor. If you make an obvious mistake at any time, one of the best face-saving maneuvers is the "self-down" mentioned in Chapter 3. You may feel embarrassed by the error, but remember that the students are also embarrassed for you. This tension can be released depending on how you handle the situation. You are in control and the students are watching. If you use self-downs regularly in your humor, your response to your mistake should be easy. For example, when I make a mistake, at least one student will catch it and say: "Shouldn't the correct answer be ___ ?" After the correction is made, my typical response is: "I can't believe this. What an idiot! How in the world did I get a job at this university? Please don't say anything to anyone or they'll fire me." As I continue raving about my stupidity, the students keep on laughing. The tension is finally broken and then I can resume the lesson to make more mistakes.

Responses to Interruptions. Finally, the last form of spontaneous humor is the ad-lib in response to outside interruptions, distractions, and physical and equipment breakdowns. Noises in the hallway or out in the street, classroom lights flickering, projector bulbs burning out, ceiling screens that won't stay down, and many other mini-disasters seem to occur in our classrooms more frequently than we probably want to recall. Consider everyone of these close encounters of the nuisance kind as an opportunity for humor. This does not mean necessarily that you always have to think of something clever and funny on-the-spot. So many professional speakers have experienced these same problems that a list of "ad-libs that aren't" has been assembled (see Chapter 3). We can now be better prepared for the next breakdown to turn it to our advantage so everyone can laugh at it. It's only a matter of time. Keep the list handy.

6. Humorous Questions

Another humor strategy you can incorporate regularly in your lectures is to ask a series of substantive questions on virtually any topic followed by one or two punch-line questions. Since a response is required, the students are forced to become involved. For those who were drifting in lalaland, the questions snap them back to attention. In my 8:30 a.m. statistics class, Monday morning no less, where falling asleep can become a habit, I use the questioning approach periodically to just keep them awake and interested. For example, on the topic of distributions and graphs, I point to graphs on the chalkboard or overhead and ask my sleepy students the following questions:

1. How many of you think this one is positively skewed?
2. How many of you think this one is negatively skewed?
3. How many of you don't care?
4. How many of you want to go back to bed?

The unexpected twist of the last two questions creates the humor, plus by forcing them to just raise their hands, I have them involved, interested, and attentive to hear the explanation that follows. Other punch-line questions include: How many want to go to lunch (or dinner)? How many don't like to be awakened during class? How many think this is a pop quiz? How many want me to stop asking these questions?

Similarly, by asking the class a simple question about their diet, whether they own a dog, or some other topic, you can prime them for the opening joke, multiple-choice item, or top 10 list on that topic. Again, they're now participants and you have their attention as you deliver the humor.

Remember to keep the responses to your questions, especially the humorous ones, easy and nonthreatening. A simple verbal or written answer or hand raising is adequate to solicit their participation in the humor. This technique will be illustrated later in this chapter in the use of *Jeopardy!* type reviews for exams. The students' written involvement in the exercise is essential to its success.

7. Humorous Examples

One of the easiest mechanisms to use humor is through the examples you present to illustrate concrete and abstract content in your subject area. There is even some evidence that students have better recall of humorous examples (Kaplan & Pascoe, 1977). The standard "serious" examples should serve as the prototypes for the structure and format of hypothetical "twisted" humorous examples or applications. Modifying a descriptive situation or scenario in a serious example can sometimes produce a jocular version. Simply using unusual names or names that create humorous images by their association with certain personalities or cartoon characters can lighten the tone of any example. A list of possible names is given below:

Males

Abdul	Clyde	Fonzy	Kipp
Alastair	Colby	Gaylord	Krishna
Aldo	Corbett	Gideon	Ludlow
Alvin	Cornelius	Gino	Ludwig
Archibald	Cosmo	Giovanni	Merlin
Attila	Dedrick	Guido	Mortimer
Barney	Demetrius	Hans	Neville
Bartholomew	Dinsmore	Hobart	Norbert
Boris	Dudley	Homer	Northrup
Bruno	Ebenezer	Icabod	Obadiah
Bubba	Efrem	Horace	Orville
Bucko	Egbert	Igor	Otto
Bunky	Elmer	Ivan	Purvis
Buz	Enoch	Jethro	Quint
Casper	Erwin	Kermit	Rolf
Cleon	Fermin	Kilroy	Rufus

Seymour	Smitty	Vinny	Xavier
Sinclair	Sven	Vito	Zebadiah
Skippy	Vern	Wilfred	Zeke

Females

Agatha	Edwina	Isadora	Pansy
Aurelie	Elsie	Lotus	Pippy
Bambi	Erma	Ludmilla	Selma
Bebe	Eustacia	Matilda	Shelby
Bianca	Godiva	Misty	Tabitha
Brunhilda	Griselda	Muffy	Ursula
Carma	Helga	Myrtle	
Chiquita	Hildegarde	Naomi	

Study the different forms of humor and the accompanying examples in Chapter 3 to build your own content examples. In addition, several examples in my boring subject area are presented next to demonstrate how humor can be plugged into almost any material. These types of humorous examples are sprinkled throughout my lectures on all statistical, measurement, and research topics. They provide "fun" examples in class that occasionally prevent some of my students' eyeballs from glazing over.

Computational Problems

Any computational problem can be transformed into a joke item by rewriting the description of the problem. The data do not have to be changed. The following problem is presented to determine whether students can choose the correct statistical tool (in this case, type of t-test), as well as set-up the solution from beginning to end:

A study was conducted to determine the relative effectiveness of two methods of teaching statistics. The first method which used JOCULARITY to teach this boring stuff was taught in the School of _____ by a promising middle-aged comedian. The second method which used traditional sadistic techniques or SAD was taught in the School of _____ by a genuine stodgy statistician. The students in each class received the same final exam. The scores are shown below.

JOC	SAD
9	3
10	1
8	5
13	6

$$
\begin{array}{cc}
12 & 2 \\
10 & 3 \\
11 & 7 \\
7 & 5 \\
\end{array}
$$

Test the difference in performance between the classes to determine whether the JOC method is superior. (*t*-test, separate variance).

Rules for Writing Test Items

Context Dependent Item

Vignette

A 25-year old white female came to the emergency room complaining of headaches, bloating, hair loss, nausea, vertigo, insomnia, hives, and green goo oozing from her ears that resembled thesis chapters. Her eyes were bloodshot and blood tests revealed high levels of caffeine, pizza, animal crackers, and beer.

These symptoms suggest the patient is probably a/an

A. undergraduate student.

B. master's level student.

C. doctoral level student.

D. A and B.

E. B and C.

F. Any of the above.

Overlapping Choices

Which one of the following expressions does The Ronmeister use most frequently in class?

A. "Good Grief!"

B. "You're NOT Going to Believe This!"

C. "Oh My Gosh!"

D. "Gotta Love Me!"

E. "I'm Gonna Hurl!"

F. A and B only.

G. B and D on Thursday only.

H. A, C, and E on the 8:30 a.m. bus.

I. None of the above.

J. All of the above.

Use of "All of the Above"

What is the primary goal of today's health care business?

A. Making money

B. Making more money

C. Making still more money

D. Making more money than "All of the Above"

Sample Rating Scale Formats

Frequency, Quality, and Intensity Item Formats

1. *Frequency*

(a) How frequently do you get the screamin' meamies per week?

Never Had 'Em	Once or Twice	Every Other Day	Once a Day	Several Times Every Day
0	1	2	3	4

(b) In conversations with your colleagues, how frequently do you use the expression "Yo!"?

Never	Very Rarely	Rarely	Occasionally	Very Frequently	Always
0	1	2	3	4	5

(c) How long do you have to sit in the waiting room to see your favorite physician?

4 10 minutes or less

3 More than 10 minutes but less than 1/2 hour

2 Between 1/2 hour and 1 hour

1 More than 1 hour but less than a day

0 I'm still waiting

2. *Quality* (Performance)

(a) How would you rate your physician's overall performance over this past year (based on 2 or more visits)?

He/She Stinks	Fair	Average	Above Average	Excellent
0	1	2	3	4

(b) How would you rate the last BIG MAC you ate?

Unsatisfactory	Mediocre	Satisfactory
0	1	2

(c) How would you rate the overall quality of the healthcare you received during your stay in this hospital?

4 This hospital's like Club Med

3 I'm still alive aren't I

2 My doctor hasn't visited me in ages

1 I look like a pin cushion

0 This hospital makes me sick

(d) How satisfied are you with the quality of care you received during your stay in this hospital?

Completely Dissatisfied	Mostly Dissatisfied	Somewhat Dissatisfied	Somewhat Satisfied	Mostly Satisfied	Completely Satisfied
0	1	2	3	4	5

3. *Intensity*

(a) "Uninflated Basketball" was an exciting addition to the 1996 Olympics in Atlanta.

Strongly Disagree	Disagree	Agree	Strongly Agree
0	1	2	3

(b) How would you rate your level of fatigue right now? (visual analogue scale)

Fresh as
a Peach _____ Like Rocky

I'm Whupped

(c) To what extent did the following slogans affect your decision to fly with our airlines?

	To a Great Extent	Somewhat	Very Little	Not at All
You Can Keep Your Airsickness Bag	3	2	1	0
We Give Two More Peanuts than Our Competitors	3	2	1	0
We Never Make the Same Mistake Three Times	3	2	1	0

Sample Likert-type Scale

Berk's Student Stability Scale (SSS)*

DIRECTIONS: The purpose of this scale is to evaluate your mental stability to withstand the rigor of this school's academic program. Indicate the extent to which you agree or disagree with each statement listed below. There are no right or wrong answers. Circle the number corresponding to your response from among the following categories:

0 = Strongly Disagree (**SD**)

1 = Disagree (**D**)

2 = Slightly Disagree (**SLD**)

3 = Slightly Agree (**SLA**)

4 = Agree (**A**)

5 = Strongly Agree (**SA**)

SAMPLE: My father was Mary, Queen of Scots. 0 1 2 3 4 5

	SD	D	SLD	SLA	A	SA
1. Earthquakes make me wet the bed.	0	1	2	3	4	5
2. It makes me angry when people bury me.	0	1	2	3	4	5

3. I often bite other people's nails.	0	1	2	3	4	5
4. My tonsils frequently come when I whistle.	0	1	2	3	4	5
5. Halitosis is a small price to pay for popularity.	0	1	2	3	4	5
6. As a child, I often suffered from bubonic plague.	0	1	2	3	4	5
7. Most people do not know how to behave in a massacre.	0	1	2	3	4	5
8. I used to collect enemas.	0	1	2	3	4	5
9. When I look down from a high place, I want to spit.	0	1	2	3	4	5
10. I prefer spiders to Brussels Sprouts.	0	1	2	3	4	5
11. I salivate at the sight of mittens.	0	1	2	3	4	5
12. I call the wind Maria.	0	1	2	3	4	5
13. Boredom excites me.	0	1	2	3	4	5
14. My mother was Erik the Red.	0	1	2	3	4	5
15. I always react to catastrophes with a song.	0	1	2	3	4	5
16. I have an urge to fondle other people's teeth.	0	1	2	3	4	5
17. I lose control when I see shoe polish.	0	1	2	3	4	5
18. Spinach brings tears to my eyes.	0	1	2	3	4	5
19. I'm afraid of being stuffed in a glove compartment.	0	1	2	3	4	5
20. I just met a girl named Mariah.	0	1	2	3	4	5

*Most of these items were adapted from A. Frankel, D. R. Strange, & R. Schoonover. (1983). CRAP: Consumer Rated Assessment Procedure. In G. H. Scherr (Ed.), *The best of the Journal of Irreproducible Results* (pp. 55-56). New York: Workman Publishing.

Sample Behaviorally-Anchored Performance Scale (Olympic Style)

Ultra-Stupendous
(Gold Medal)

| Leaps tall buildings in a single bound. | Is more powerful than a locomotive. | Is faster than a speeding bullet. |

Kinda Better Than Ordinary
(Silver Medal)

| Leaps short buildings in two or more bounds, maybe. | Can draw a picture of a locomotive. | Is about as fast as a speeding BB. |

Middling Garden-Variety
(Bronze Medal)

| Leaps short buildings with a running start and a strong tailwind. | Can pick out the locomotive in an H-O train set. | Tries to catch speeding BBs in teeth. |

Putrid
(Pet Rock)

| Barely leaps over a Port-O-Potty. | Says "Look at the choo-choo!" | Wets self while shooting a water pistol. |

Sample Research Hypotheses

Sample Hypotheses	Statistic
• There will be *significant positive* relationship between sunscreen protection factor and intelligence of the user.	Correlation (directional, 1 tail)
No. of Samples: ____	
No. of Variables: ____ ; ____ ____	
• Level of stress will accurately *predict* the annual rate of hairballs of doctoral students.	Simple Linear Regression
No. of Samples: ____	
No. of Predictors: ____ ; _____	
No. Criterion Variables: ____ ; _____	

- Among the variables of verbal   Multiple Regression
  ability (VA), quantitative
  ability (QA), undergraduate
  GPA (UGPA), and payoffs to
  the Dean, VA and UGPA will
  most accurately *predict* success
  in the master's program.

  No. of Samples: ____

  No. of Predictors: ____ ; ____ ____ ____ ____

  No. of Criterion Variables: ____ ; ____

- Students who regularly eat   *t*-test (Separate variance)
  the "Roadkill-of-the-Day   (directional, 1 tail)
  Special"from the cafeteria will
  have a *significantly higher*
  degree of heartburn than
  students who eat at Hot Dog
  Hilda's on 33rd Street.

  No. of Samples: ____

  Method of Assignment: ____

  Independent Variable: ____ ; ____ ____

  Dependent Variable: ____ ; ____

- Men who use the new   *t*-test (Repeated Measures)
  medication "Snow Removal"   (directional, 1 tail)
  to eliminate dandruff will have
  significantly less dandruff on
  the Snow Removal Scale after
  two months.

  No. of Samples: ____

  Method of Assignment: ____

  Independent Variable: ____ ; ____ ____

  Dependent Variable: ____ ; ____

- There will be a *significant*   Chi-square Test of
  difference in the incidence   Independence
  of athlete's foot, back pain,
  and varicose veins between
  shoe salespersons and other
  types of salespersons.

  No. of Samples: ____

  Method of Assignment: ____

  Independent Variable: ____ ; ____ ____
  ____ ; ____ ____ ____

Sample Research Proposal Skeleton

Problem/Research Question

1.0 Are the three major cold remedies really different in their effectiveness to relieve cold symptoms?

Hypothesis

1.0 There will be a significant difference among the cold remedies — Triamine®, Triayours®, and Triatheirs® — for sneezy-coughy students in terms of degree of relief.

Methods

Research Design: Pretest-posttest control group, quadruple blind experimental design

Independent Variable: Brand of cold remedy (3 levels)

Dependent Variable: Degree of relief (or cold remedy effectiveness) as measured by the Phlegmwad Cold Symptom Relief Scale (Phlegmwad, 1993)

Sample

Baccalaureate student volunteers at the *(name)* University School of *(name)* will be solicited to participate in the study. A total of 150 students with cold symptoms will be selected using Kleenex Screening Test. This sample will then be randomly divided into three groups of 50 each. The cold remedies will be randomly assigned to the groups.

Instruments

The Phlegmwad Cold Symptom Relief Scale will be used to measure the presence of a variety of cold-related symptoms, including stuffy nose, sneezing, coughing, gagging, projectile vomiting, gout, kidney stones, and halitosis. The scale is a self-report device that requests the respondent to identify the presence and degree of discomfort or misery associated with each symptom. The symptom is rated on a continuum of 0–5, using the anchors "Not Present," "Present and Accounted For," "Slight Discomfort," "I Hate This," "This Makes Me Really Mad," and "My Kids are Going to be Punished for Giving Me This Cold." The total score range possible for 20 symptoms is 0 to 100, where 0 means no symptoms ("Happy, Happy, Joy, Joy!") and 100 means supermiserable (☹).

Reliability and validity evidence has been reported previously on comparable samples of college undergraduates by Nyquil (1991), Sneezy, Sleepy, and Stuffy (1995), Robitush (1996), and Ludens and Hacking (in press). Gamma Delta Kappa reliability coefficients ranged from .78 to .91.

Procedures

The scale will be administered to all students on a mass transit bus Monday morning. They will then be given a bottle of medicine labeled A, B, or C. No one will know the brand each student is assigned; not even the researchers. (This procedure is designed to eliminate experimenter bias.) The concentration of each medicine was calibrated so that the dosage was standardized for all three brands: one time-release suppository every 12 hours. The measurement of degree of relief over time and across the three different brands required that the Phlegmwad Scale be administered every 48 hours over a two-week period.

Statistics

Hypothesis 1.0 will be tested using a 3 x 7 factorial analysis of variance. One factor is the independent variable of brand of cold remedy; the second factor is the repeated measures over the two weeks. Newman-Keulade or Roast Turkey's Test for pairwise comparisons will be used to detect the most effective cold remedy and the point in time when that effectiveness occurred.

Sample Dissertation Title Page

HOMICIDAL MANIACS REALLY MEAN WELL:

REHABILITATION OR DECAPITATION

by

Jack T. Ripper, Jr.

DISSERTATION

Submitted to the School of Phlebotomy of Freddy
Krueger University

in partial fulfillment of the requirements for the
degree of

Doctor of Philosophy

Toad Sphincter, Utah

May 2001

Sample References in American Psychological Association (APA) Format*

Barby, B., & Kenn, K. (1971). The plasticity of behavior. In B. Barby & K. Kenn (Eds.), *Psychotherapies R us* (pp. 34–67). Detroit: Ronco Press.

Boleyn, A., & Antoinette, M. (1660). Quit while you're a head. *Guillotine Reports, 8,* 116–118.

Brady, C., & Partridge, S. (1972). My dad's bigger than your dad. *Acta Eur. Age, 9,* 123–126.

Chaney, L. (1925). Phantom of the operating room. *Archives of Perpetual Care, 9,* 90–99.

Dork, U. R. A. (1991). *Memoirs of Steve Urkel.* Chicago: Family Matters Publications.

Dracula, C. (6–5000). *Everything you always wanted to know about sleep deprivation but were afraid to ask.* Paper presented at the annual meeting of the International Vampires Association, Transylvania.

Flintstone, F., & Jetson, G. (1994 B.C.). Cognitive mediation of labor disputes. *Prehistoric Industrial Psychology, 2,* 23–35.

Ford, H. (1992). *Jerusalem Jones and the lost afikomen.* Cairo (NOT!): Pyramid Press.

Gabor, Z. Z., & Taylor, L. (1981). Marriage: Institution vs. tradition. *Annals of Bad Habits, 40,* 23–26.

Heinz, C. (1991). Use of the "plugged-up ketchup bottle" metaphor in educational research. *Journal of Condiment Behaviors, 12,* 66–91.

Ivy, P., & Oak, P. (1991). *Invasion of the body scratchers.* Philadelphia: Benadryl & Calamine Brothers Publishing.

Joe, G. I. (1965). Aggressive fantasy as wish fulfillment. *Archives of General MacArthur, 5,* 23–45.

Keaton, A. (1990). Money: The family tie that bonds. *Sitcom Rerun Quarterly, 85,* 234–240.

Knot, Y. (1975, May). *Extinction of learned behavior.* Paper presented at the annual meeting of the Siberian Psychological Association, Kamchatka.

Moe, R., Larrie, T., Kirly, Q., & Shemp, C. (1984). Spontaneous remission of childhood. In W. C. Fields (Ed.), *New hope for children and animals* (pp. 234–256). Hollywood: Acne Press.

Piggy, M. S. (1990). *My needs are simple but my wants are simply extravagant.* Orlando, FL: Muppet Productions.

Popeye, T. S. M. (1968). Spinach: A phenomenological perspective. *Existential Botany, 35,* 908–913.

Prepared, B. (1963). Human behavior as a model for understanding the rat. In M. de Sade (Ed.), *The rewards of punishment* (pp. 921–963). Paris: Bench Press.

Presley, E., & Houdini, H. (1988). I'm in touch, so you be in touch. *Oak Lawn News, 17,* 240–344.

Rogers, F. (1979). *Becoming my neighbor.* New York: Sweater Press.

Seuss, D. R. (1983). A psychometric analysis of green eggs with and without ham. *Journal of Clinical Cuisine, 245,* 567–578.

Spanky, D., & Alfalfa, Q. (1978). Coping with puberty. *Annual Review of Aquatic Psychiatry, 6,* 45–46.

Spielberg, S. (1993). Octogenarian dinosaurs who gum each other for fun and profit. *Geriatric Park Quarterly, 2,* 65–71.

*Several of these references were adapted from J. W. Smoller. (1985). The etiology and treatment of childhood. *Journal of Polymorphous Perversity, 2* (2), 3–7.

8. Humorous Problem Sets

The same approach used to prepare the preceding in-class humorous examples can be applied to the development of humorous problem sets on any topic. They can supplement or provide an alternative to the typically "serious" textbook problems. The problem sets can be assembled as handouts and assigned to the students as in-class practice problems, small-group problem-solving exercises, or homework. This strategy can extend the humor you used to illustrate particular points in class to the students' own learning experiences in class and in their home environments. It tests their ability to apply methods and concepts taught in class to completely new generic, albeit humorous, problem situations. A few "serious," content-specific problems may also be included in the problem sets to reinforce the generalizability of their skills.

9. *Jeopardy!* Type Reviews for Exams

The development of this strategy stemmed from the difficulties my graduate students were having on one specific section of their midterm exam. This problem occurred several years ago. Obviously the format of my review was not effective. I adapted the *Jeopardy!* game-show format to the items used in the test reviews for the following semester's class. Compared to the previous class' performance on the test section in question, this semester's class test scores skyrocketed. Since then, all reviews for all tests in all of my classes are in, guess what format: *Jeopardy!* Best of all, I get to play Alex Trebek.

There are two books on *Jeopardy!* (Trebek & Bersocchini, 1990; Trebek & Griffin, 1992) that I discovered in a bookstore while on summer vacation that provide tons of examples of *Jeopardy!* "answers." I highly recommend reading at least one of these books to get the feel of how to word "answers" for content you want to review for a test.

First, list the basic content you want to cover in the review. Knowledge level content is the easiest to adapt to the *Jeopardy!* format; however, application and even evaluation level material can be used. Then convert the content into *Jeopardy!* answers with humorous cues when possible. For presentation to the students, the category is given first, followed by the item answers, all in *Jeopardy!* boxes of course. Each item is given on a blue transparency and the students write their question on a prepared answer (or rather question) sheet. If there are 10 items in one category, all may be completed before reviewing the correct "questions" on the answer sheet or the students can respond immediately after each item. Try both formats to determine which one works best with your students. Examples of a few categories and items are shown below:

Types of Distribution and Graphs

Where most students perform well on an exam and only a few blow it; also something used with shishkabob.

(What is a negatively skewed distribution?)

This graph consists of bars with no gaps to represent continuous variables; also a Western Union message sent by a snake.

(What is a histogram?)

Picking the Correlation

This type of correlation between overall GPA at graduation and passing/failing the *Where's Waldo?* Licensing Exam (1,0) also expresses the relationship between Frosted Flakes and Fruit Loops.

(What is a biserial correlation?)

This type of correlation between graduating or not graduating the program (1,0) and employed versus not employed (1,0) was also the first (and second) sound Jack heard on the beanstalk.

(What is a phi coefficient?)

This type of correlation should be computed between vampires' quantity of blood consumed per night and their monthly orthodontics' bill.

(What is a Pearson correlation?)

This type of correlation should be used between Schmeck Depression Inventory scores (0-100) and Prozac or Tictac patient medication classification (0,1).

(What is a point-biserial correlation?)

This type of correlation measures whether marital status (single, divorced, married, looking) is associated with educational level (high school, street wise, bachelor's degree, *Jeopardy!* finalist).

(What is a contingency coefficient?)

This type of correlation between two judges' rankings of athletes' balance beam performance also sounds like a brand of gum.

(What is Spearman's rho?)

After all of the items have been completed and reviewed, it's time for *Final Jeopardy!* I usually pick a category and item with which some students have previously experienced difficulty or confusion. Of course, it is introduced using Trebek's words: "You will have 30 seconds to write your question to this answer. *(answer read)* Good luck!" *Jeopardy!* music is played and the students love it. An example is given below:

Final Jeopardy!

Stepwise Multiple Regression

This is the 2nd BEST predictor of ADMISSION into the Master's Program based on the following correlation matrix:

Predictor	2	3	4	5	6	ADMISSION
1. Eenie	.61	.78	.82	-.59	.18	.43
2. Meenie		.75	.56	.33	-.29	.91
3. Meinie			-.42	.21	.35	.88
4. Moe				.50	.66	.72
5. Schmoe					.27	.55
6. Bloe						-.76

(What is Bloe?)

The entire *Jeopardy!* review requires about an hour of class time to cover the material for each test, which students report on their course evaluations to be time well spent.

10. Humorous Material on Exams

There are four elements in a test where humor can be inserted: (1) title, (2) directions for taking the test, (3) test items, and (4) last page. The humorous material is designed to decrease the students' tension, stress, and anxiety levels in order to maximize their performance.

Title. The cover page provides the first opportunity to use humor. The humor on this page can have the most significant impact on the students' psychological state before answering the first test question. The descriptors recommended previously for syllabi and other handouts should appear under the title of each test. Choose totally incongruous descriptors from the list provided. For example, "BAKED

WITH PRIDE" for the midterm and "DOLPHIN SAFE" for the final can be very effective. This element alone guarantees at least a smile and usually more.

Directions. Similar to the above, encountering jocular directions on the first or second page is an unexpected twist that can really release tension. Suppose you read the following directions on your midterm:

General Directions

The purpose of this test is to find out whether you know anything.

Place the ANSWER sheet somewhere in front of you. Using the little pencil you kept from your last miniature golf game, print your name, social security number, and test booklet number in the upper right corner so we can track you down. Read the directions for marking your answers.

You may do computations in the test booklet or on a separate worksheet, because if I said, "DO NOT MARK IN THE BOOKLET," you would probably do it anyway.

Answer all questions as best as you can. There will be no penalty for guessing, so have a blast. You will have the entire class period to complete the test.

DO NOT begin the test until you are told to do so or you can be hurt.

For the final you can get even bolder:

General Directions

Sit down and shut up.

Place the ANSWER SHEET somewhere in front of you. Print your name, social security number, and test booklet number in the upper right corner so we can track you down. Read the directions for marking your answers.

Answer all questions as best as you can. There will be no penalty for guessing, so have a blast. You will have the entire class period to complete the test, which means you have 1.25 minutes per question.

DO NOT begin the test until you are told to do so or you can be hurt. I'm going to let you sit here and sweat

for about 30 minutes before letting you start the test.
You are allowed to breathe; but nothing else.

Test Items. The section with the greatest jocular potential is the test items themselves. Unfortunately, for years I was led to believe that humor on tests should be used sparingly. Most measurement textbooks written over the past 25 years suggest including maybe one or two joke items on a test to keep students awake and inject a little levity into what is a rather stressful situation (see, for example, Mehrens & Lehmann, 1991). A few professors of measurement have reinforced this notion. Several years ago as I was developing humorous material to reduce anxiety in my statistics classes, I discovered a few research articles on the psychological and physiological benefits of laughter and humor (see Chapter 1). Eureka! (Literally means, "I'm having reflux.") It struck me that probably the highest levels of tension, stress, and anxiety that students experience during a course occur while taking tests.

Restricting humor to a couple of items ignores the evidence on the potential power of humor to reduce anxiety and stress during those times. A few studies conducted in the 1970s have even provided preliminary data to conclude that exposure to humorous test items can significantly reduce anxiety in very anxious students (Adams, 1974; Berk & Nanda, 1997; Smith et al., 1971). However, McMorris, Boothroyd, and Pietrangelos's (1997) comprehensive review of research on using humorous test items indicated inconsistent findings on anxiety, worry, stress, and performance, despite students' preference for humor on tests. The authors encouraged the use of humorous items, especially if humor is included in instruction, the test has a generous time limit, the humor is positive and constructive, the humor is appropriate for the students, the students come from the same culture as the professor, and the professor feels comfortable in using humor.

The "serious" test items can be converted into humorous items following the same humor formula used to develop the humorous examples and problem sets described previously. Humor formats are most effective for application, analysis, synthesis, and evaluation questions. In other words, they fit items that measure cognitively complex and higher-order thinking skills. The humor is least applicable at the lowest level of cognition for items that test knowledge by recognition or recall.

One of the disappointments that can occur with developing humorous test items is that you receive very little feedback on whether the humor was successful or had any effect on the students' performance. During the exam, you usually see a few smiles and may hear an occasional chuckle, but rarely a chortle. These reactions do not provide overwhelming reinforcement for the time spent creating a jocular test.

Only on end-of-course evaluations and studies of the effectiveness of humor (Berk, 1997a; Berk & Nanda, 1997) will you find that students perceive that humorous test items decrease their anxiety and increase their ability to perform at their best.

Last Page. Finally, a humorous note on the last page of the test can end the grueling test- taking experience with a smile. It's a kind of cooling down jocular exercise or mirthful debriefing. Here are a couple of notes you can use on different tests:

> NOTE: This was only a TEST. If this had been an actual emergency, you wouldn't be sitting here suffering through this stuff. You may now resume your regularly scheduled activities.
>
> or
>
> NOTE: This test was made possible by a grant from the Society for the Prevention of Cruelty to Statisticians (or any other group) (No. YA-GOTTA-LOVE-ME!)

Chapter 7

Using Humor in Professional Presentations

As professors we serve in a variety of capacities outside of the class-room, one of which requires that we make formal presentations. These presentations may occur at teaching and research conferences, work-shops, meetings, hockey games, Lamaze classes, and Tupperware par-ties. They often take the forms of research papers, didactic or training sessions, critiques, committee reports, keynote or plenary speeches, infomercials, and confessions. The audience may consist of peers in our discipline, professionals in other disciplines, administrators, policy makers, students, the lay public, aliens, livestock, or any combination of the preceding.

Among those presentations you have made, approximately how many would be considered "deadly" by those sitting in your audience? Now be honest. Over the past 25 years, about 65% of mine would fit that description. In fact, the other 35% occurred only within the past decade. How could I be so boring? Was it because of the low expecta-tions of the audiences to tolerate humorless, colorless, undramatic pre-sentations in deference to the substantive messages I delivered? (*Interocular Observation:* Professors have an extremely high threshold for tolerating deadly presentations by their peers.) Was it due to my lack of training in basic techniques of public speaking and communication, despite the appearance of courses in those areas on my transcripts? Or, is it simply that with all of my commitments, there was no time available to focus on "how" I present since it was only the "what" that counted anyway? Or, maybe, I was just a lonely, insecure, boring person. Just kidding! It is ironic that most of what we are paid to perform as professors requires formal speaking in teaching our classes, conducting and participating in meetings, and reporting our research results. Yet many of us have the charisma of linoleum and generate as much excitement in our presentations as a root canal.

When I was a professorial fledgling, I always admired the speaker at my annual research conference who could use humor in his presentation. (I never witnessed a "her" attempt humor until about 10 years ago). Keep in mind there were very few of any gender who were successful in their jocular efforts. (*Note:* The use of whimsy at my annual conference occurred at about the same frequency as the Hale-Bopp comet.) As a member of the audience, I thought to myself, "I wish I could do that, but it seems really scary. What if the joke bombs? I'll look like an idiot. How embarrassing it would be to fail in front of my peers."

A couple of years later I finally gathered up enough nerve to take the plunge. In the course of my presentation, I made a deliberate effort at humor. The audience's response was, to put it bluntly, nonexistent. There was no visible response or sign of life, no audible sound of a chuckle, much less a guffaw. The audience may have been on life support. Heeellooo! Welcome to BOMBING 101.

Maybe I'm really slow to grasp certain concepts*, but one day I finally realized that the net effect of bombing in front of any audience is the same as though no joke was ever told. When you bomb, you may feel embarrassed or humiliated, but, in most cases, the audience probably couldn't tell the difference. *Total silence is the norm for the overwhelming majority of boring presentations delivered everywhere.*

Based on a self-assessment that my presentations were as stimulating as the test pattern of the Emergency Broadcast System, I decided to reverse this disastrous course. I developed a variety of techniques that involve "low-risk" humor as opposed to the "high-risk" stand-up joke I was hesitant to tackle (see Chapter 3). I devised a 20-step process to contextualize the creation, execution, and critique of humor within the entire presentation framework. This framework is similar to a construction project to build a presentation laced with humor. All 20 steps or only a few may satisfy your needs for integrating humor into your presentation.

1. Prepare the "WHAT" Well in Advance

"WHAT" you have to say is the reason for the presentation. It is the content, substance, meat, pancreas, and the slimy, plaque-clogged, faintly-pumping heart of your lecture and what the audience is expecting and

*My wife and daughters can attest to my "grasping impairment."

usually paying to hear. People are not attending your presentation to listen to a stand-up comic, although they probably wouldn't leave if you were really funny.

The objectives of your message should drive the structure and triple by-passed heart of the presentation. It should be so well-planned and organized that your audience can easily learn what is presented without the humor. That is, it needs to be outlined and fleshed out early in your preparation to permit adequate time to focus on "HOW" it is going to be delivered. Whether the "WHAT" is the results of your research, a topical address, a committee report, or a prenuptial agreement, all of the substantive information should be specified in a form ready for presentation. Although minor changes are expected up until the last minute, you should not be writing the main content on the night before or the morning of the presentation. Subtle HINT, HINT, HINT, HINT!!!

2. Prepare Handouts of Key Points

Handouts can guide the audience through the presentation and keep them awake. Print material in front of every person is one of the most effective mechanisms for involving your audience in the presentation and maintaining their interest and attention. Force them to do something beyond just providing them with handouts to follow the key points. Make them fill in salient information, take notes on important thoughts that strike them, interact with persons on each side to share ideas or solve problems, or physically attack each other at regular intervals during your presentation. Numbered lists with blanks will require them to write down the ideas they hear and/or see on the overhead transparencies or slides and concealed weapons attached under the seats can be used for small combat exercises. These activities produce participants rather than spectators and can reduce drifting, napping, idle chatter, snacking, and cross-dressing.

3. Plan "HOW" the Presentation Will Be Made

Start thinking about methods for presenting the products of steps 1 and 2. This process should continue until the moment that the presentation begins. One of the major distinguishing characteristics of presentations given by professors, administrators, researchers, politicians, business executives, religious leaders, and ChemLawn guys is "HOW" the information is conveyed. These professionals, as well as many others who are required to speak to a variety of audiences, often consume so much time in the preparation of the "WHAT" that there is little or no time to prepare the "HOW." In fact, some of these professionals do not consider the "how" that important. That is a serious mistake. Get real! Rarely do you find an audience that can be expected to be sitting on the edge of their pelvic bones awaiting every olive of wisdom you spew. Professional "motivational-type" speakers, such as Zig Ziglar, Peter Lowe, Tom Hopkins, Les Brown, and Attila the Hun divide their preparation time between the "WHAT" and the "HOW." We need to study the methods they use to deliver their powerful messages.

Be conservative in judging the interest level of your audience in "WHAT" you have to say. I always make three fairly safe assumptions: (1) the content I present is incontrovertibly, indisputably, and undeniably BOOORING; in fact, it is prescribed regularly in lieu of Valium for patients at Johns Hopkins Hospital, (2) the people in the audience would probably prefer to be somewhere else, such as Bermuda, Sri Lanka, or the New Jersey Turnpike, and (3) they are concentrating on their personal agendas and items of immediate importance to them, such as baseball, pyorrhea, soybeans, or the dead bugs in the front porch light fixture, rather than on what I am presenting. Although I have never actually surveyed my audiences on the content of the mental baggage they dragged into the room where I am speaking, I suspect the preceding assumptions are justified. That says I have to work extremely hard to persuade, to convince, or to sell my message or, at minimum, to find techniques to prevent members of my audience from experiencing whiplash, or even snapping their necks, as they keep dozing.

Since we have all been exposed to presenters who have read their papers, don't even think about it. Consider the points to be made and how they can be transmitted most effectively. Use your imagination and creativity to carve out your own path. You can certainly start with "safe" methods, but you should also experiment. Do something unusual that your audience will remember and, also, appreciate.

4. Determine the Size of the Audience and Physical Characteristics of the Room

Initially, collect data on all of the typical unknowns in your presentation and turn them into knowns to take advantage of the physical layout in how the speech is delivered. Certainly the preparation involved for a ballroom/auditorium that seats 2000 people, a theater-style lecture hall that accommodates 300 people, a 20-seat conference/board room, and a 1-seat port-o-potty would be quite different. Although there are some forms of humor, such as stand-up jokes or anecdotes, that will work in almost any setting, there are others that are limited by physical restrictions, such as costumed skits and cartoons.

Obtain information on the estimated size of the audience and the physical characteristics of the room, such as size, acoustics, lighting, stage or podium, arrangement of seats, trap doors, air composition (oxygen to cologne ratio), temperature (climate controlled at 150 F.), goal posts or basketball hoops, radiation protection, and plastic sneeze shields on the buffet tables. You might also want to inspect the flooring if the room has been used for tractor pulls and direct-mail conventions.

Humorists indicate that, in general, *the larger the crowd and more tightly people are packed into a room, the greater the response to humor.* Laughter stimulates other laughter. Consider Ed "Publishers Clearinghouse Sweepstakes-Star Search-Colonial Penn Life Insurance" McMahon's role on Johnny Carson's *Tonight Show* and Kevin Eubank's function, besides band leader, on Jay Leno's *Tonight Show.* Their infectious laughter cued the audience to laugh. People are encouraged to laugh when others around them are laughing. The trick is to get enough people to laugh to infect the borderline laughers to let loose.

Laughter is maximized by the size of the audience and, more importantly, by the arrangement of the people. If only 20% of your audience can be expected to laugh at one of your jokes, this translates into 2 in a group of 10, 10 in a class of 50, and 100 in an audience of 500. There is a greater chance that the 100 laughers will encourage many of the remaining 400 to laugh than the 2 affecting the other 8 in a small group of 10. The factor of size alone can make a big difference in the response to your humor.

However, whether people are crowded or spread out in a room is even more crucial to your success. Smooshing people together yields more positive responses to humor than spreading them out. Fifty people in a room designed for 50 or 60 will be more responsive to humor than the same 50 distributed all over a room that accommodates 250. Wright and Wright (1985) have identified four reasons why crowding enhances an audience's response to humor: (1) it produces numerous potential laughers whose laughter can encourage borderline laughers to laugh, (2) it creates tension when people are packed in like sardines and laughter affords an opportunity to release that tension, (3) it improves the speaker's image, as people see a packed room, which suggests he or she must be good, and, therefore, they tend to be receptive, and (4) it creates the impression that more people are laughing due to resonant acoustics; that is, the more echo in a room, the greater the response to humor.

Given the significance of size and crowding, what can you do when you walk into the room for your presentation and 50 people are spread out in an auditorium that holds 250? Pass out toads that secrete an hallucinogenic substance they can lick while you're speaking. Ha ha. That's probably not an appropriate first step, because before you know it, they'll be hurling themselves into the walls and onto the stage like wildebeasts on Dexedrine, which can be very distracting to those people without tongues. It would probably be better to request the audience to move to the front and closer together to increase "intimacy" and so they can hear and see you better. Any strategy you can think of to concentrate the audience close to you will increase their responsiveness to your humor. For example:

> "If you have an IQ greater than a dish of potato salad, please move down front and center."

> or

> "If you want to avoid contact with the disease-ridden vermin living under the seats in the back of room, it is recommended that you move to the front."

> or

> "To those of you sitting on the end seats near the aisles, you should know that the people who sat in your seats yesterday were apparently exposed to a bacteria that produced a major outbreak of zits. You might want to consider moving in toward the center."

5. Conduct a Comprehensive Profile of Your Audience

Probably the most important determinant of the success of your presentation is the extent to which you are able to tailor your remarks to the needs and wants of your audience. It is essential that as much information as possible be obtained about the characteristics of the audience, including age, gender, race/ethnicity, professional experience, institutional affiliation (e.g., college/university, federal, state, or local government agency, private industry, military), position (e.g., professor, student, administrator, practitioner), content or technical expertise, conviction-to-acquittal ratio, and food preference (carnivore, herbivore, or Jenny Craigivore). This information is usually available from the conference organizers, parole officers, Covert Bailey, or other officials involved in arranging your presentation.

The distribution and combination of characteristics that comprise your audience profile represent the target for the substance and humor you present. A very common error that accounts for many "deadly" speeches and humor that "bombed" is simply not knowing the audience. Knowledge of the audience profile is essential in order to develop appropriate humorous material. One single characteristic, such as years of experience in a minimum security facility, date of last tetanus shot, or lactose intolerance, can be the difference between the success and failure of your humor.

6. Review the "WHAT" for Opportunities to Use Examples and Illustrations

Perhaps the easiest vehicle for incorporating humor into any presentation is the "example." This strategy was described previously in the context of classroom applications (see Chapter 6). Although the content or information may be serious, the way in which it can be illustrated or applied doesn't have to be. Depending on the content, you may have enough time to use both humorous and serious examples. A humorous example can also serve to emphasize or exaggerate an important point that may not be possible with a "real" example. The joke example or cartoon not only injects some levity into the presentation, but can also serve as a teaching tool. A jocular visual image can have a stronger impact and, sometimes, longer effect on learning than a serious content illustration.

Your task at this stage is to determine what types of examples can be developed and where they can be placed in the presentation. What content could benefit from an example, illustration, or application of some kind? Identify "serious" material that could be used at key points in the presentation to furnish examples.

7. Develop a Pool of Humorous Examples

Use the "serious" examples to provide the structure and format for hypothetical, "twisted" humorous examples. Other formats include multiple-choice items, top 10 lists, one-liners such as quotations or questions, riddles, cartoons, and animal illustrations. The sources of humorous material identified in Chapter 4 and the formats illustrated throughout the other chapters can furnish a ton of material and ideas that can be adapted to a variety of content examples and illustrations.

Draft several humorous examples for each point being illustrated. This pool of examples should not be distributed to the audience as part of the handouts. It will constantly change as new examples are added, "bombs" are discarded, and semi-winners are revised to become winners.

Extract only the absolute BEST examples from the pool to include in your presentation. If you are not sure, don't include it in a reeeally important presentation to a large audience. One or two bombs can detract from the winners.

8. Prepare a Humorous Introduction

The initial impression the audience receives of you begins before you even say a word. Once you are introduced, the audience rivets their eyeballs on every movement you make. So be careful. There are three simple gestures you can demonstrate from the moment you're introduced that will set the tone for what follows, which will be your humorous introduction. Below are three generally acceptable behaviors and three unacceptable ones just for comparison.

Acceptable Behaviors	Unacceptable Behaviors
1. Walk quickly to the lectern with a smile to convey your enthusiasm and delight to be there to speak	Drag your sluggard self to the lectern with your head down and an angry expression on your face, grumbling nasty words under your putrid breath
2. Shake the hand of (or hug) your introducer and thank him or her for the introduction	Punch your introducer in the stomach, then lean over while he or she is gasping for air and whisper, "I'm going to blow up your car after the conference"
3. Greet the audience with "Good morning/afternoon/ evening"	Greet the audience with "In your face you bunch of low-life scumballs"

Those acceptable behaviors, which can take less than a minute, project to your audience the warmth, cuddliness, and furriness of Tickle Me Elmo. The unacceptable ones project the charisma of cow phlegm and the intelligence of Mayonnaise-lite. Take your pick. Which image do you want to start your presentation? You say, "Neither." Okay. Well, maybe you'll like the humor options below better.

Although speakers are almost always told to give a positive first impression by telling a stand-up joke to warm up the audience, that approach has become predictable, trite, and, for some presenters, unrealistic. Use humor that fits your personality and speaking style. If you possess the skills to deliver a joke with the timing and body language needed for a successful response, do it. However, not everyone can tell jokes well. It is "high-risk" humor that depends on both good material and dramatic delivery. Instead of taking a chance on a punch line that may not work, which is not the best way to begin a presentation, there are several alternative "low-risk" techniques that you can use. Ten different methods that have been tested under a variety of conditions are described next.

a. Humorous Biosketch. If you want the audience to see you as a humorist, one strategy is to supply them with a brief humorous biosketch. I experienced the effect of this technique when I attended a benefit presentation by humor columnist Art Buchwald. As I walked into the theater and searched for a seat, many people who were already seated were laughing, and Buchwald wasn't even in the room. (I bet you thought they were laughing at me. Not this time!) I started reading the program and soon understood the source of the laughter. Buchwald's biosketch was a scream. What a simple yet powerful tool to prepare your audience for a fun presentation.

This strategy provides the information the audience wants to get to know you, plus it is written humorously. The "bio" can be distributed with the handouts for your presentation. It serves three important functions: (1) you are certain the key background information on your credentials is presented accurately, (2) you have set a humorous "fun" tone for the entire presentation, and (3) you have removed an enormous burden from the shoulders of the person who is to introduce you, so he or she only needs to make a few remarks. Selected lines from my biosketch are given below as an example:

> _Ronald A. Berk_ is Professor of . . . and Jester-in-Residence at the _____ University. In addition to his PhD, he has a license to practice jocularity from the Chuckle Institute for the Humor Impaired. Prior to begging _____ University to hire him, he taught . . . This experience changed his life forever. He then completed a three-year stint . . . where he developed a strong aversion to memos and meetings. Professor Berk has admittedly contributed to the destruction of scores of trees and shrubbery by publishing . . . He is a past president of . . . and served on the Council's Board of Directors . . . His election to these positions totally shocked his parents who expected him to have his own talk-show by then. His most recent research . . .

b. Cautions and Warnings on the Cover of the Handout. Similar to the preceding strategy, you can place humorous material on the cover of the handout package so the audience can read it prior to your introduction. This is exactly the same technique described in the previous chapter for classroom handouts. A few choices from the list of cautions, warnings, and information in Chapter 6 can be very effective. In addition, since I usually put a copyright seal on the cover of my training course handouts, the following humorous "WARNING" can be given on the second page:

> **WARNING:** These materials are protected by U.S. copyright laws, whose enforcement you and I both know mean diddlysquat! There's a better chance of Mr. Ed winning the Kentucky Derby than of a federal marshall (or even Walker, Texas Ranger) busting you for copying my jokes. So, anyway, nothing in this handout may be reproduced, stored in a retrieval system, frozen, shredded, or transmitted in any form or by any means electronic, mechanical, photocopying, recording, paranormal, or otherwise, without the prior notarized written permission of Moi. (Yeah, right!)

Another "WARNING" which is a parody of an actual warning at the beginning of most books can also be presented just after the cover page:

WARNING: The receipt of this paper without its cover is unauthorized, unsanctioned, uncensored, unbelievable, and not very nice. If you received this paper without a cover, you should be aware (but not necessarily care) that it was reported to the author as "stripped" (a.k.a. naked as a jay bird). Neither the author nor the sponsor of this presentation has collected any dough from the distribution of this uncovered counterfeit version, but then again, we're not talking about big bucks for the authentic version either.

These unexpected items on the cover and/or second page coupled with the humorous biosketch leave no doubt in the minds of the audience that this presentation is going to be fun. The stage has been set without saying a word, much less a "high-risk" joke. Now that the humorous tone has been set, you are expected to be funny. So be prepared to deliver.

c. Questions About the Composition of the Audience. After you're introduced, one technique to find out about your audience (although you should already have a preliminary profile), to get them involved in the presentation, and to maintain your humorous tone is to ask three or four simple questions to which they respond by raising their hands. I have seen this questioning method used very effectively by Joseph Stowell, President of the Moody Bible Institute in Chicago. He tailors his questions to the variety of audiences he addresses. It is an extension of the same basic in-class questioning technique described in Chapter 6, just adapted to different types of audiences. An example of a series of four questions is shown below:

(1) How many of you are college professors?

(2) How many of you are administrators?

(3) How many of you work in a local or state government agency?

(4) How many of you don't like quizzes by your speaker?

or

(4) How many of you don't want me to ask any more questions?

The first three questions request valid information, but then the fourth, which is the unexpected twist, becomes a punch line.

This technique can be used effectively at appropriate points during the presentation as well. For example, if you are going to move into a section on technical material and you're not sure of the levels of expertise in the audience, a sequence of questions such as the following may be used:

(1) How many of you have had at least one course on . . . ?

(2) How many of you recall the basic concepts of . . . ?

(3) How many of you don't care?

(4) How many of you want to go to dinner?

d. Humorous Disclaimers. Disclaimers are placed on just about every product and service purchased. So why not put disclaimers on your presentation? Again, it's the unexpected twist as part of a substantive message that makes the disclaimers humorous. Taking standard cautions, warnings, and disclaimers out of context with a jocular spin to boot produces the humor. Two or three disclaimers may be listed on the second or third page of the handout or presented on an overhead transparency or slide. Introduce the list as follows:

Lead-in: "It seems appropriate to list my disclaimers for this presentation before I begin so there are no false expectations." Pause for about 15 seconds for the audience to read the list. An example is given below:

DISCLAIMERS:

1. All of the characters in this paper are fictitious. Any resemblance to actual persons — living, dead, or somewhere in between — would be purely coincidental and reeeeally bizarre!

2. No animals were harmed or mistreated during the preparation of these materials, although the theme from *Free Willy* was played during the production of the transparencies.

3. Don't perform any of the suggestions in this paper at home. You must be a trained professional like me. If my suggestions seem blatantly stupid, potentially injurious, disrespectful to all forms of life, or outright dangerous, it's because they probably are.

A list of several other disclaimers that you can use as is or "humorize" similar to the above is presented below:

- This paper is void where prohibited, taxed, or otherwise restricted, and no purchase is necessary.

- This paper is guaranteed to be free of any physical defects, design flaws, and poor workmanship.

- The paper must be used only for its intended purpose and in accordance with manufacturer's specific warning.

- In no event shall I be liable to anyone for specific, collateral, incidental, or consequential damages in connection with or arising out of purchase or use of these materials.

- Information in this paper is subject to change.
- The content in this paper is subject to change without notice.
- Warranty does not cover accidental damage, misuse, misapplication, or damage resulting from modification or service other than an authorized service center.
- Liability for loss or damage of this paper is limited, unless a higher value is declared in advance and additional charges are paid.
- The warranty on this paper does not cover misuse, accident, lightening, flood, tornado, volcano eruption, earthquake, and other Acts of God, neglect, damage caused by improper installation, improper or unauthorized repair, missing or altered serial numbers, blasting by mine crews, jack-hammering, or sonic boom vibrations.
- The user takes full responsibility for everything and anything that could and/or does go wrong resulting in any kind or type of problem, difficulty, embarrassment, loss of money or goods or services or sleep or anything else whatsoever.
- Warranty is NOT valid if incident occurs owing to an airplane crash, ship sinking, motor vehicle crash, fallen rocks, leaky roof, broken glass, mud slide, forest fire, or projectile (which can include, but is not limited to, arrows, bullets, buckshot, BBs, shrapnel, lasers, napalm, torpedoes, emissions of X-rays, Alpha, Beta, or Gamma rays, darts, knives, stones, etc.)

e. Acknowledgment of Funding Sources. Another opportunity to juxtapose the expected with the unexpected is to acknowledge the funding sources for the research related to your presentation. However, it's the legitimate (serious) premise or lead-in of searching for funding sources coupled with absolutely ridiculous sources that makes the combination humorous. Pick three or four sources from the list below or create your own.

Lead-in: "I attempted to obtain federal funding to support the research and data analysis for this presentation. Unfortunately, no agency would provide any financial support, and once you hear this presentation, you'll probably understand why. However, I pounded the pavement in Washington, DC, and finally got partial support from several institutions. I would like to acknowledge the following:"

Ridiculous Sources:

Moisha & Izzy's Bagel Shop

Chickens that Almost Crossed the Road Café

Beenie Weenie's Carpet Cleaning

Leroy's Bait & Tackle

Arnie's House of Controlled Substances

Wuf & Puf Speed Eating Clinic

Helga's Tattoo and Taco Parlor

Buford's Bulldozer Repairs

"Bazookas R Us" Weapons Discounter

National Society for the Prevention of Cruelty to (Statisticians)

Slick Rick's Bail Bonds (Freedom While-U-Wait)

Guido's Rid-Your-Relatives Pest Control Service (For In-Laws Who Overstay Their Welcome)

Jack-in-the Box Drive-Thru Funeral Parlor (When You Care Enough to At Least Show Up)

The sources should be read and revealed one at a time using an overhead transparency. Consider each source as a punch line. The more absurd the source, the more effective the humorous impact.

f. Generic Joke or Anecdote. A prepared joke in multiple-choice format or top 10 list on a topic with which everyone can relate is another alternative to the "high-risk" joke. These formats were described and illustrated in Chapter 3. Localize your material to the sponsoring agency, organization, or corporation, conference city or town, officials, laws, airport, etc. to personalize the humor for your audience. That will provide a friendly linkage between "outsider" you and the audience. It demonstrates an interest in them and conveys to them from the beginning that you are not going to deliver an impersonal canned presentation. For example:

Lead-in: "As I flew into ____ airport last night, I'm still amazed at some of the things these airlines say to you on your flights. They have their own language and I don't think it's English. I'd like to take a moment to show you a few examples of "airlineze":

Item: Which one of the following expressions by the airlines is an OXYMORON?

A. Complete stop

B. Direct flight

C. Nonstop flight

D. Airline food

After concluding that the answer is "D," play off of the literal meaning of a few of these expressions compared to the airlines' meaning, such as: "As the aircraft taxied to the gate, a thought occurred to me.

Can someone please explain to me the difference between stopping the aircraft and coming to a complete stop?" (Pause) "Isn't that somewhat redundant? May I ask you another question while we're on this topic? "How many of you have actually been on a *nonstop flight?*" (Pause) A few people will usually raise their hands. I say to them "You wouldn't be here! You would still be circling indefinitely!"

An example of a localized multiple-choice item adapted from parts of one of Letterman's top 10 lists (Letterman et al., 1991, p. 106) is shown next. Note that the content of the item is restricted to one season of the year and major filthy, crime-ridden cities:

Lead-in:　　"It's so great to be here in Baltimore at this time of the year. To give you an idea of some of the wonderful sights here, I like to see whether you can answer the following question:

Item:　　What is the most obvious sign of spring in Baltimore?

　　　　A. Garbage collectors start going topless.

　　　　B. A dog-size rat emerges from the sewer to look for his shadow.

　　　　C. There's a dramatic increase in the number of murders committed with gardening equipment.

　　　　D. Lovely pastel colors are used for chalk body outlines.

If your presentation is being sponsored by a specific corporation and many of the leaders and members are in the audience, you can poke fun at the organization with a top 10 list. For example:

Lead-in:　　"Although there's a lot you know about (<u>organization</u>) from working with their staff, there may also be a few things you don't know and probably should know. For example, I bet you are anxious to know what T-shirt expressions were seen last summer at (<u>organization</u>) annual picnic. Based on my highly reliable snitch, I was able to assemble the Top 10 T-Shirt Expressions Seen at the (<u>organization</u>) Picnic. You might even be able to match the expressions to the employees here today."

Top 10 List:

Top 10 T-Shirt Expressions Seen at the (Organization) Picnic

10. Friends Don't Let Friends Move to Bosnia

9. My Wife Says I Never Listen to Her — at Least That's What I Think She Said (Donna Wafer)

8. I'm a Liberal Arts Major - Will THINK for Food (Jay Tortona)

7. One Tequila, Two Tequila, Three Tequila, FLOOR (Samantha Lockwood)

6. Never Play Leap Frog with a Unicorn

5. I Attended the Seattle Rain Festival (Jan. 1 – Dec. 31) (Judy Colbert)

4. Always Remember You're UNIQUE, Just Like Everyone Else

3. Hukt On Foniks Wurks for Me

2. Help Stamp Out Intolerance

1. Illiterate? Write for Help

A true "funny" story can also be told as a lead-in to the topic of the address. A story is "low-risk" because it's not a set-up with a punch line and the audience can relate their own experiences to yours. Your success in telling the story doesn't hinge on the laughter. Truth is in, concocted jokes are out (Hoff, 1992). However, the story should be practiced so that the delivery is polished. (See Chapter 3 for several examples, Chapter 4 for sources you can consult, and Chapter 5 for techniques for delivery.)

g. *Quotation from Children's Book or Humorist*. Another technique that can be very effective is a quotation that conveys a feeling or context for the presentation topic. What creates the humor in this situation is the contrast between the lead-in remarks and the source of the quotation. The quotation itself may also be humorous. One example is given below. It was drawn from one of Joseph Stowell's presentations.

Lead-in: "Like all of you, I try to keep up with the scholarly research and literature in my field. Representing an academic institution, I thought it would be appropriate to search for a meaningful quotation in the literature that may capture the feelings that some of you may be having. I finally found one. According to Dr. Seuss (Geisel & Geisel, 1990):"

Quotation:

You'll be on your way up!

You'll be seeing great sights!

You'll join the high flyers who soar to great heights.

You won't lag behind, because you'll have the speed.

You'll pass the whole gang and you'll soon take the lead.

Wherever you fly, you'll be the best of the best.

Wherever you go, you will top all the rest.

Except when you *don't*

Because, sometimes, you *won't.*

I'm sorry to say so

but, sadly, it's true

that bang-ups

and hang-ups

can happen to you.

You can get all hung up

in a prickle-ly perch.

And your gang will fly on.

You'll be left in a Lurch.

You'll come down from the Lurch

with an unpleasant bump.

And the chances are, then,

that you'll be in a Slump.

And when you're in a Slump,

you're not in for much fun.

Unslumping yourself is not easily done. (pp. 11–19)

h. *Lyrics from a Popular Song.* Based on an idea suggested by Dave Barry (1988, p. 68), selecting reeelly ridiculous and stupid lyrics from a song with which most people are familiar can be used to convey your excitement or enthusiasm for being at the conference or the key theme or message you are going to address. The contrast among the serious build-up in the lead-in, the actual unexpected stupid lyrics, and the reinforcing serious remarks after the lyrics provides the elements for a humorous introduction. Two possible lead-ins are given to introduce the lyrics:

Lead-in: "It is just a delight for me to be here with you today to give this keynote. Probably the best way I can truly express my excitement is through those memorable lyrics from Liza Minnelli's smash song *New York, New York:*

or

Lead-in: "I've put a lot of thought into what I'm going to present here today. I have concluded that there seems to be one driving theme that is the foundation of my message. Probably the most eloquent way I can express that theme is through those memorable lyrics from Liza Minnelli's smash song *New York, New York:*

Lyrics: Dum dum da de dum

              Dum dum da de dum

Dum dum da de dum

Dum dum da de dum dum.

Transition: "What else can I say? What a powerful message those words convey." (*Optional:* "That message is even more profound when played at weddings and bar mitzvahs.")

i. Organization of Presentation. Many presentations can be conveniently organized into three sections, such as introduction, middle, and finale. This provides an opportunity to play on the three-phenomena notion with humorous examples. Again, it's the legitimacy of the rationale for organizing the presentation into threes stated in the lead-in that is juxtaposed against "unusual" examples that creates the humor. A standard lead-in with a list of examples from which you could pick any "three" are suggested below:

Lead-in: "This presentation is organized into three sections (parts or prongs). The justification for this has been the significant life forces (or phenomena) throughout history that have occurred in threes, such as:"

Examples: The Holy Trinity

Gaul

Three Dog Night

3 Rocks from the Sun

Three Million Dollar Man/Woman

Three's Company

My Three Sons

The Three Stooges

Rambo III

Rocky III

Superman III

Police Academy III

Poltergeist III

The Three Amigos

Three Leagues under the Sea

Star Wars Trilogy

3 Ninjas Knuckle Up

Star Trek: Deep Space Three

The 3rd Wives' Club

Three Men and a Baby

Three Blind Mice

Snow White and the Three Dwarfs

Goldilocks and the Three Bears

Tic Tac Toe

Dickens' *A Tale of Three Cities*

The Three Musketeers

The House of the Three Gables

Newhart's buddies — Larry, Darryl, & Darryl

j. Skits and dramatizations. If the topic of your presentation can be linked to the *Star Trek,* "Tool Time," or *Mister Rogers'* skit described in Chapters 3 and 6, or any other skit that you have created, give it a shot. Since we "act " in front of our classes day in and day out, this jump to a precisely written, choreographed, rehearsed, and acted skit as the lead-in to your substantive message is not that far.

The size of the effort to design and execute a skit will be dwarfed by the size of the impact on the audience. The skit is such a strong visual and verbal statement as well as clever method to introduce any topic that it can leave an extremely positive and lasting impression on your audience. They will definitely remember your rendition of Tim "The Tool Man" Taylor. Depending on how you execute it, they may never forget it. The skit is a feature of your presentation that sets you apart from other speakers.

Also consider the significant advantage we have as professors compared to other academicians or speakers. We have an easily accessible training ground on which to hone our acting skills. Any skit I have developed has been practiced numerous times in my classes before using it with any audience of my peers or other professionals. You can keep polishing the material and delivery as many times as needed until you feel you are sufficiently prepared for the big time.

9. Design a Humorous "Finale"

A presentation that begins with humor and sustains the expectation of humor throughout the speech with examples should end with humor. The challenge is to be creative, provide a "twist" on the key points or a summary that will be both informative and humorous. There are five suggested techniques worth considering: (1) "new television shows you might want to watch that relate to the topics covered," (2) "recent movies on cable (or in your hotel room on Spectravision) to learn more about the topic," (3) "new techniques or methods that have just been published that you will want to try," (4) a step-by-step top 10 list, Letterman style, from your home office wherever, or (5) a *Jeopardy!* quiz summarizing the important concepts.

All of these methods build on the actual content summary. List the main points, practical applications, step-by-step procedure, etc. that tie the entire presentation together. Now comes the hard part. How can these key points be expressed as TV shows, movies, new methods, a top 10 list, or *Jeopardy!* answers. Most any procedural summary can be squished into a top 10 format which may not be funny, but it still works well as a finale. The *Jeopardy!* review described and illustrated in Chapter 6 can be used to review the important elements of your presentation. The other three formats are more difficult to develop. Examples of the movie concept, new methods, top 10 list, and *Jeopardy!* quiz are shown below:

Movie/Video

The purpose here is to put a humorous spin on several popular movies to reinforce the terminology and concepts of several characteristics of performance assessment, including portfolios, structured interviews, assessment centers with in-baskets, high-stakes versus low-stakes decisions, scoring rubrics and benchmarks, and holistic versus analytic scoring methods.

> Which one of the following hit videos on performance assessment is now available in your hotel room on Spectravision?
>
> A. The story of a dedicated music teacher's 30-year search for criteria to score his symphony...
>
> *MR. HOLLAND'S RUBRIC*
>
> B. A young basketball player aspires to be a pro as an assessment center in the documentary...
>
> *IN-BASKET DREAMS*
>
> C. The story of National Geographic photographer Robert Kincaid and the standards he uses to score with an Iowa farm wife in...
>
> *THE BENCHMARKS OF*
> *MADISON COUNTY*
>
> D. Tom Cruise's application of performance assessment in Transylvania...
>
> *STRUCTURED INTERVIEW WITH*
> *THE VAMPIRE: A HIGH-STAKES DECISION*
>
> E. The Steven Spielberg story of a fantasy island where a team of performance assessment scorers attain perfect reliability...
>
> *HOLISTIC PARK*
>
> F. The story of a creative teacher and his secret performance assessment club that meets in caves...
>
> *DEAD PORTFOLIO SOCIETY!*

New Methods

The following item is a parody on a few widely used statistical methods. It's a fun finale for a statistical presentation with a statistically sophisticated audience. The stem can be adapted to a variety of situations. The one below would fit nicely into a presentation before Christmas or Hanukkah.

> Which one of the following NEW STATISTICS would make a wonderful gift for the quantitatively-minded researcher?
>
> A. MULTIPLE AGGRESSION ANALYSIS or MAA! for researchers with a Napoleon or Oedipus Complex
>
> B. DISCRIMINANT LUNCHEON ANALYSIS for gourmet researchers who just love to classify people
>
> C. MANOVA/WOMANOVA for multivariate researchers from Mars/Venus
>
> D. SCHEFFÉ AU LAIT, the multiple comparison choice of neo-yuppie researchers
>
> E. DECAFFEINATED T-TESTS, available in assorted flavors, for researchers who get their jolt from pairwise analysis

Top 10 List

This top 10 list is a combination format I devised to conclude a technical presentation on setting standards. I wrestled between an "awards" approach and a top 10 list. So I combined the two into an effective finale. Also, given the pessimistic tone set my the "number 1 award," I added a memorable quotation from one of my favorite television series to lighten it up a bit.

Lead-in: "My summary of the main points of this paper is an awards presentation expressed as a top 10 list. So, from my home office in Baltimore, MD, here are the top 10 awards for standard-setting methodology:"

Top 10 List:

> 10. *Most Promising Old Approach:* Multistage Iterative Process
>
> 9. *Most Promising I/O Psych. Approach:* Behaviorally Anchored Scaling
>
> 8. *Most Politically Correct Procedure:* Selecting a Broad Based Panel of Judges
>
> 7. *Most Politically Incorrect Procedure:* Using Only Content Experts to Set Standards
>
> 6. *Most Confusing New Term:* Polychotomous or Polytomous

5. *Most Psychometrically Incorrect Procedure:* Asking Unqualified Judges to make Uninformed Decisions

4. *Most Challenging Old Procedure:* Consensus Building Among Judges

3. *Most Challenging New Complication:* Setting Multiple Cut Scores

2. *Most Neglected Technical Topic:* Evidential (Predictive) Validity

And the number 1 award for

1. *Most Difficult to Defend:* (Goes to) All of the Above!

As Sergeant Phil Esterhaus of *Hill Street Blues* used to say to his officers every morning, "Hey, let's be careful out there!"

"Jeopardy!" Quiz

The *Jeopardy!* format can be presented as a pop quiz to summarize important concepts and information. The administration should be nonthreatening to the audience and must conclude with *FINAL JEOP- ARDY!* The example shown below was used to summarize the psychological and physiological effects of laughter and the characteristics of humor from one of my training courses on humor.

Lead-in: "In order to assess whether you learned anything in this session, I'm going to give you a pop quiz, which means it's time for *Jeopardy!* This morning's category is"

Characteristics of Humor

"After each answer is presented, shout out the question. Are you ready? Let's begin."

Jeopardy! Answers:

1.
> Your body releases this chemical substance when you laugh and also exercise; it could decrease the pain of listening to Moi.

(What are endorphins?)

2.
> This major psychological effect of laughter is also produced by eating junk food.

(What is reduce stress?)

3.

> This important physiological effect of laughter may make you less susceptible to catching mononucleosis and other exotic diseases.

(What is build up your immune system?)

4.

> Humor can REDUCE this feeling in students during teaching and, especially, before exams; also the title of a Mel Brooks movie.

(What is high anxiety?)

5.

> This type of humor is totally inappropriate in a teaching-learning context; also what you become when you don't use deodorant.

. (What is offensive humor?)

6.

> This is the number of elements in most forms of humor and also the number of bears who mauled Goldilocks.

(What is 3?)

7.

> This is the final element or stage of any joke which Jay Leno and David Letterman deliver nightly.

(What is the punch line?)

8.

> Knowing the characteristics of this is critical to the success of your humor; there would be no laughter without it.

(What is your audience?)

9.

> This is usually what happens when your joke doesn't work; Bob Hope has "dropped" a lot of these.

(What is bomb?)

10.

> This theory of humor focuses on bigger than life targets, such as the institution, practices, and policies; also what can result from eating too many Twinkies.

(What is "Big Butt?")

Lead-in: "It's now time for"

Final Jeopardy!

"The category is"

Thinking Humorously

"You will have 30 seconds to write your question in big letters on your sheet of paper to the following answer:"

> When you're in doubt about any joke being offensive to your audience, focus the joke on this to be safe.

(What is yourself?)

"Good luck."

(Play *Jeopardy!* theme music)

"On a count of 3, hold up your question and shout it out. One, two, three..."

10. Practice Presentation to Estimate the Time

Rehearse your presentation to estimate the time. Remember, there may be laughter, but don't factor that in your estimate. Be conservative. There are at least five phenomena to consider that may justify shortening your presentation: (a) your actual presentation usually tends to be longer than your rehearsed version, (b) the conference begins late, (c) the speaker schedule is behind and you may be expected to end on time regardless, (d) the person introducing you goes on longer than expected, or (e) there is a blackout, earthquake, alien invasion, or nuclear explosion that may put a slight crimp in your time allotment.

11. Adjust Humorous Material to Fit Within the Allotted Time

The most common presentation times for professional presentations are 10–20 minutes for research presentations, one hour for keynote addresses, and two to four hours (or one to three days) for training sessions. Based on your previous estimate, adjust your introductory humorous material and examples, not the content, accordingly to fit your total presentation into less than the time you were assigned. The substance of the presentation should be firm unless you are trying to cover too much. In that case, it may be necessary to trim content as well as the humor.

Check with conference organizers to determine whether there is any latitude with the time limit. If you are the only speaker or if the presentation is in the evening just before the audience goes to dinner, use your best judgment. If you're not sure about the timeframe, be empathetic with your audience. Yield to the possibility that many of the participants may have just endured a miserably long flight with maybe 4 measly peanuts. They're probably on the verge of starving to death. If you dare drone on incessantly under those circumstances, expect to be murdered in your bed that night or, at minimum, to find the head of a musk oxen under the covers.

12. Insert Humorous Material into Content

Beyond the introductory humorous material, humorous examples woven throughout the content, and humorous finale, there is one more opportunity to integrate humor. Scrutinize the serious dull, boring content itself to determine whether a word, a phrase, or a box in the theoretical model can be altered with something humorous that will lighten the material a bit and emphasize a particular concept. Humorous terminology can be more effective and yield greater recall of details than the heavy content as long as it doesn't distort or detract from the substance. Be careful not to derail the train of thought you have created with inappropriately placed humor.

A graphic illustration of boring material on types of assessment tools conceptualized along a continuum was improved by inserting some jocular in-jargon into the boxes in Figure 2. It not only elicited smiles and laughter from the audience to break up the serious content, but it communicated strong, colorful distinctions among the categories that emphasized the concepts. Further, the nontechnical audience to whom I was speaking could easily relate to the terms as they were applied to technical issues.

13. Edit Humorous Material to Assure It Is Not Offensive to Anyone

The premise regarding the use of offensive humor is that any humor that could offend anyone is totally inappropriate. This topic was discussed at length in Chapter 3 and the recommendations given in that chapter apply to professional and lay audiences as well as students.

Continuum of Assessment Tools

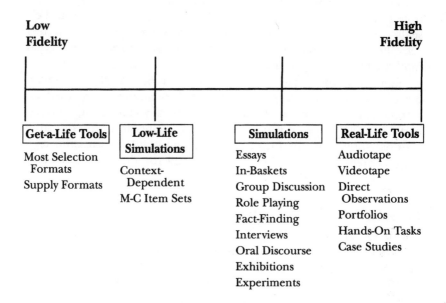

Low
Fidelity

High
Fidelity

Get-a-Life Tools	Low-Life Simulations	Simulations	Real-Life Tools
Most Selection Formats	Context-Dependent M-C Item Sets	Essays	Audiotape
Supply Formats		In-Baskets	Videotape
		Group Discussion	Direct Observations
		Role Playing	Portfolios
		Fact-Finding	Hands-On Tasks
		Interviews	Case Studies
		Oral Discourse	
		Exhibitions	
		Experiments	

14. Assess the Distribution of Humorous Material

Steps 7, 8, 9, and 12 generated humorous material throughout the presentation. It is time to carefully evaluate the distribution of that material to answer the following questions:

(1) Is the humor woven throughout or is it clumped in certain spots only?

(2) Is the humor appropriate for its content placement in the presentation?

(3) Is there a strong humorous beginning and a big humorous finale?

(4) Is this the dumbest thing I've ever done, or what?

The answers to these questions should indicate the necessary adjustments.

The distribution of humor over the entire presentation is crucial to maintain audience interest and attention. Interject some juicy tidbits into the presentation at regular intervals, such as every seven minutes. (I just made that up.) It has been said that "humor is like a diaper change — it makes you comfortable for a while." A pattern of humor provides intermittent reinforcement of humor which will motivate your audience to stay alert and snap back to attention any wandering minds. It also serves as a change of pace. Wright and Wright (1985) noted that "the period of laughter allows the listeners to shift in their seats, to get the blood and oxygen circulating again, and to feel refreshed. Like a cool drink on a hot day, it can rejuvenate them and motivate them to stay with you" (p. 29).

Remember the humor is being used as a tool to facilitate communication of your message. As the distribution of humor is examined, be certain that the collection of humorous material you have chosen is the best "sure-fire" material you have available. Untested or questionable material should not be included in an important presentation to a large audience. If it is, always be prepared for the worst response, although it may not occur.

15. Select Your Audiovisual Aids

Decide exactly what audiovisual materials, equipment, and props you need to execute your presentation. The advantages and disadvantages of the various types of aids that can be selected to facilitate your humor as well as the rest of your presentation were examined in Chapter 5. Weigh that evidence against the humor formats you have chosen and the physical characteristics of the room in which you will present. Make sure your equipment requests were received by the organizers of the conference.

Lastly, when you arrive at the conference site, remember to verify your requests and to test all of the equipment and props in advance, if possible, even your tool belt or sweater and sneakers. If you have access to the room prior to your "production," check all electronic equipment to make sure the projectors, VCRs, television monitors, computers, and/or microphones work and you know how to operate and handle them. Fumbling with the lavaliere microphone or searching for the on-off switch on the projector is not the best way to kick off your otherwise meticulously planned presentation.

Also check the alignment and focus of all projector images on the screen with your own transparencies and slides and the room lighting required to read the material clearly on the screen from different positions in the audience. Your standard-type homo sapien audience should not need specialized equipment, such as telescopes, periscopes, and satellites, to see the projected material. Make all adjustments before your production begins. Your careful preparation on all preceding and succeeding steps in this process will not be evident if your transparencies are out-of-focus or keep falling off the projector and you are constantly tripping over your microphone wire. The true mark of a professional is to be over-prepared so nothing is left to chance. Now I bet your thinking, "Does that mean I must be super-compulsive and anal-retentive about my preparation?" Let me make sure I understand this. We are now at the end of step 15 in this seemingly endless, excruciatingly painful process to inject humor and some zip into your presentation, and you're wondering about whether this is compulsive behavior? You bet your bippy it is. Okay, it's time to get back to our story about tripping over wires. The issue is: no matter how much you prepare for smooth audiovisual effects during your presentation, as professors, we also know "Murphy's Law" is applicable to everything we do, especially presentations that are really important to us. I usually manage to pull off my presentations with an average of only 38.33 glitches.

16. PRACTICE, PRACTICE, PRACTICE Your Delivery

The presentation should flow naturally like your body on a number 4 white-water rafting trip. The only way a performance of any kind appears natural, spontaneous, effortless, and authoritative is by hours of practice or lots of retakes and editing if you're being videotaped. Given the amount of humor integrated in the presentation, the timing and intonation of the "jokes" are especially important. Since virtually all of the "low-risk" techniques described previously with accompanying examples can be prepared on overhead transparencies or slides, there is nothing to memorize. In fact, only anecdotes require memorization. However, all humorous material needs to be delivered with the proper timing and dramatic effect, and that requires practice. Review all of the recommendations for an effective delivery presented in Chapter 5. Also, note the strategies for recovering from a bomb, just in case.

17. Retain a Pool of Backup Humorous Material That Can Be Substituted at the Last Minute

Take backup jokes, cartoons, and other humorous material in a separate file to your presentation. Sometimes after listening to some of the other speakers or just seeing the audience, you immediately may have the sense that a few of the jokes are not going to work or you're in the wrong hotel. If any of your planned material seems inappropriate once you've arrived at the conference site, pull it. Go to your backup file to substitute appropriate material if it is worth substituting. If not, leave it out of the presentation. Don't take a chance with material that is questionable for any reason.

18. Edit Humorous Material Prior to and During the Presentation

Continue reviewing the material in terms of the actual audience profile sitting around you. If you misjudged the age, gender, or species distribution, discard those "dentures," "testosterone," or "weasel" jokes.

Once you have begun your presentation and the audience has responded to the first few jokes, consider editing your remaining material based on the early returns (a.k.a. audience response or lack thereof). Leno and Letterman edit their prepared jokes and skit material almost every night. After they hear the audience's reaction to the first couple of jokes, you will notice them skipping over others. Political humorist Art Buchwald developed his own system to draw on jokes that match the audience's response. He keeps his stories on color-coded index cards, with each color representing a different category of story. When he begins a speech, he tells one story from each color. The story that gets the biggest laugh is the category he selects for the rest of his presentation.

You know your best material and you've rehearsed the presentation to be able to count on certain winners. If the "winners" are not succeeding, what's going to happen to the other material? Yooou know! When you get to those parts of your presentation, simply keep moving, retain those jokes that you want, and skip over others. Remember, the audience can't tell the difference because their handout package contains only the substantive content, not the jokes. You have complete flexibility to change, add, or subtract humorous material at any time prior to or during the presentation.

19. Celebrate Your Successes, But Conduct a Postmortem ASAP

Whatever happened, you probably weren't boring. Enjoy the positive feedback and repress the negative at least for a little while. Within 24 hours of your victory, conduct a complete autopsy of the humorous material to assess what did and did not work. You may have won the war, but not every battle was a winner. Recall audience reaction to each item and punch line. A cassette or videotape of the presentation would be extremely helpful to pinpoint the specific successes and failures. Guestimating why certain material didn't work is essential to improving the material, even though different audiences tend to respond differently to the same material.

There are three key areas to examine that usually account for most bombs: (1) the humorous material itself, (2) the audience profile, and (3) your delivery. The one-liners used in prepared examples in multiple-choice or top 10 format may be true or clever, but simply not funny. Anecdotes may have the same problem or they may be too long or too short. If the material doesn't work after one presentation, don't give up. It may be successful with a different audience.

The mismatch between the humor and the audience profile is one of the most frequent explanations for bombs. The "commonly understood situation" is essential for all forms of humor and it is easy to misjudge the audience's knowledge or familiarity with the material in your humor. Professional humor or "in-jokes" are particularly susceptible to this error. Age, gender, and professional experience are also very common factors in explaining why certain material fell flat.

Finally, if your material and audience don't seem problematic, it could be your delivery. Trace through the list of recommendations for an effective delivery in Chapter 5 to identify where you may have faltered. It could be one or a combination of factors to which you can attribute your failure.

After this analysis, repair the damage by revising the material and/or improving your delivery while the content and audience response are fresh. Consider most of the humorous material always to be in a constant state of revision. Jokes in whatever format can almost always be improved. Incorporate the new and improved versions into your humor pool for future presentations.

20. Continue This Process Forever

Repeat steps 1–19 for your next presentation and continue this process indefinitely or until you land a comedy-writing job on Leno, Letterman, Seinfeld, etc., whichever comes first.

Chapter 8

Using Humor in Publications and Communications

All of the preceding chapters focused on presenting or performing humor in front of your students, professionals, lay audiences, or various low-life creatures featured on *The Discovery Channel*. But then you already knew that unless you just skipped illegally to this page searching for the surprise ending. Surprise! Surprise! There isn't one. This chapter concentrates on how to transform what you deliver into what you write. Certain types of humor you perform may be less effective in written form or not effective at all. Many of the prepared "low-risk" techniques described in Chapters 3, 6, and 7 were designed for visual impact, such as quotations and questions, cartoons, humorous examples and problem sets, and humorous material on syllabi, exams, and other handouts (e.g., descriptors, cautions, warnings, disclaimers, directions, and funding sources). Some of these will pack a stronger punch when delivered orally and visually.

Those methods should provide a starting point for generating humorous ideas that can be integrated into different types of written material: (1) professional publications, such as articles, chapters, books, living wills, and appliance warranties, (2) academic communications, such as memos, e-mail, faxes, graffiti, and bumper stickers, and (3) other formal documents, such as meeting agendas, TIAA/CREF reports, travel expense forms, golf tournament registrations, traffic tickets, and restraining orders. The strategy for inserting humor into this variety of material is the same as that employed for classroom and professional presentations: Write the "WHAT" first. Then search your imagination for "HOW" you can bring it to life with jocular material.

One major difference between humor in an oral presentation and humor in print is that the latter will be subject to the scrutiny of editors, reviewers, critics, conference organizers, and colleagues everywhere, some of whom will have the understanding of a tackling dummy and lurk in the shadows waiting to pounce on every jocular effort you produce. Of course, there will also be a few who will be supportive, encouraging, and appreciative. Unfortunately, your humor must be salable to all of these professionals based on *their* criteria, which may not be the same as yours.

This chapter is divided into three thongs. If thongs are able to keep your feet from slipping out of those spongy beach sandals, they should restrain you from slithering out of this chapter. Those thongs are: (1) humor salability factors, (2) published and unpublished vehicles for humor, and (3) humor in academic communications and documents. Before you dive into the issue of salability, cerebrate on the following semi-deep thought:

> **CAVEAT PROFESSORUS/AE**: Your creative efforts to apply humor to various print and electronic media may be less difficult than obtaining its acceptance and appreciation by those for whom it is written. In other words, if you thought rejection in the scholarly publications domain was depressing, writing humor for professorial readerships can drive you to order Zoloft by the case, plus it can get you into more professional trouble than all of the preceding presentation techniques combined. So if you thrive on rejection and professional insecurity or you have tenure, which means you can only be removed with nuclear weapons, you've stumbled onto the right chapter. Read on, Othello (or was it Iago?).

Thong 1: Humor Salability Factors

There are four key subthongs that can determine the salability of your humor in "serious" professional published and unpublished works: (1) type, (2) form, (3) quality, and (4) quantity.

Type. By definition, written humor is "low-risk" from the perspective of our self-esteem, but risky in terms of professional acceptance. There will always be colleagues who will put down your use of humor as inappropriate, degrading, and demeaning to the profession. But who cares? That never deterred me before when they said that about my research contributions. Even the most creative, imaginative, and nonoffensive humor can receive that type of response. It will be a no-win proposition with many fellow professionals. Considering the fact that you will hit the wall with this segment of your audience and possibly lose some of your professional credibility (e.g., not taken seriously because of your humor), you need to weigh those losses against the benefits of using humor. Many professionals will respect, admire, applaud, envy, and even lust after your jocular efforts for producing a delightful change of pace from the overwhelming serious and boring material they're used to reading.

Here you have an opportunity to break the mold of the super-serious scholar-researcher to become (would you believe...) a role model and set an example of how to use humor tastefully and appropriately in your substantive contributions to the field. Remember the content of your written message remains intact. You have simply decided to communicate differently from others by using humor. In this context, obviously all of the previous warnings regarding offensive humor are reinforced and even more stringently applied, if that's possible.

Form. The form of humor is determined to a great extent by the content of your work. Humorous examples, cartoons, and references must relate to the substance. Other generic forms mentioned previously can be applied to almost any scholarly topic. Quotations, descriptors, cautions, and warnings can be placed under the title; disclaimers can appear in the introduction or in a footnote; and humorous funding sources and acknowledgements would, of course, be presented as footnotes.

There are other forms that are specific to writing humorously. They differ in their simplicity or complexity and are a function of the humor skills of the writer. These forms include: (a) colorful, graphic, and figurative language, (b) lists, (c) sidebars, (d) footnotes, (e) warnings, and (f) personal style.

The simplest form is language that creates funny images in the minds of the readers. Using *figurative language*, such as graphic metaphors and similes, *non sequiturs*, and *popular expressions* throughout a serious text can relieve boredom, stimulate your readers' interest, and maintain their attention. For example, instead of writing "Those results were very surprising (or shocking)," use "Those results blew me off my beach chair"; or instead of stating "Those conclusions are discouraging," use "Those conclusions made me feel lower than a slug's belly"; or use the ubiquitous "Helloooo!" or "Yeah right!" in a strategic location. Hundreds of colorful expressions can be found in Larsen's (1995) book. Other examples of ones I have used are sprinkled (rather than "can be found") throughout this book, such as military metaphors and slogans ("humor bootcamp" and "BE ALL THAT YOU

CAN BE") and slightly altered Trekkie expressions such as "This book ... boldly goes where no professor has gone before!" Perhaps one of the most widely used and effective language forms is hyperbole. Exaggeration of any characteristic to the level of absurdity that the reader knows it isn't true will usually produce at least a chortle. The "Big Butt" Theory of humor mentioned in Chapter 3 is an example of this concept. The exaggeration is especially applicable to self-effacing humor, which is used frequently by professional humorists, such as Dave Barry. You have probably concluded it is one of my favorite attempted forms of humor as well.

Lists of almost any serious content can be twisted into humor breaks in the text. Simply tack on absolutely ridiculous items at the end of a list. This technique follows the incongruity formula of humor by presenting the reader with expected serious items and then, all of a sudden, the unexpected twist of absurd and bizarre items follow providing one punch after another. I consider virtually every list in this book as fair game. For example, the introduction to the book and the introduction to this chapter presented three lists of examples of written material where humor can be injected: publications, communications, and documents. In both introductions the first few real examples were similar, but the ridiculous examples were different just to have fun with those lists. Obviously the challenge is to create the punch items. Only one to three are necessary to lighten up the text.

There are at least three advantages to using this form of humor: (1) the serious, comatose content remains intact, (2) the punch items do not distract from the substance, yet provide needed jocular relief, and (3) the list gives the illusion of a lot of substantive material, when, in fact, there is barely any.

Sidebars are unexpected and, hopefully, funny comments inserted into the text for the same reasons as above. Since they're basically wisecracks or editorial remarks and are usually irrelevant to the content, they should be set off in parentheses. I use these comments frequently to reduce boredom in my own writing, especially when the material is really heavy or technical. Sidebars can lighten the tone a bit. Their main disadvantage is they interrupt or distract from the flow of the text. That is essential to the humor; the sidebar is an unexpected break in the expected serious content. The sudden interruption creates the incongruity necessary for the impact. Unfortunately, some readers may find that annoying. In fact, you may already be annoyed by my use of them.

Footnotes serve as an alternative mechanism when sidebars may be too disruptive to the text. The humorous comments are essentially the same; it's just a matter of where they should be placed on the page. Footnotes may be less effective than sidebars because many readers pay less attention to them and, sometimes, ignore them completely. For that reason I use them infrequently.

Warnings within the text are nothing more than glorified comments set off from the text, preceding the paragraph or section to which it refers. It warns the reader of something ominous or strange about the upcoming content. Dave Barry uses "Reader Alerts" in several of his books for the same purpose. Since they are purely for entertainment and do not interrupt the flow of a paragraph, they can be very effective and welcome mirthful interludes.

For lack of a more explicit term to capture all of the other tools humorists use in their writing, I have chosen *personal style*. There are characteristics of written expression unique to every writer that demonstrates the rare ability or gift to transform ordinary substantive thoughts into extraordinary "twisted" humorous words that produce laughter. These are possessed by the professional humorists who write syndicated humor columns daily, weekly, and monthly in hundreds of newspapers and magazines. You probably have your favorites. You already know mine: Art Buchwald, Dave Barry, the late Erma Bombeck, and Leo Tolstoy. Their humorous writing styles applied to a zillion legitimate and illegitimate topics serve as examples we can study and emulate. The more I read their columns and big fat books, the more I want to be like Mike. If you are unfamiliar with their work, I heartily recommend them if you want to embark on this new hobby or career direction. As noted in Chapter 4, the best place to begin on your own is to copy the style of your favorite comedian or humorist. Eventually your personal style will emerge.

There are very few examples of humorous writing styles in academic disciplines. During my career in methodology, I know of only one author who has consistently displayed a gift for writing humorous articles and texts in educational measurement — my mentor, Jim Popham, a professor emeritus at UCLA for centuries and founder and director of his own private test development contracting firm (IOX Assessment Associates). I have a hunch the opportunities are wide open for you to cut a new humorous path in your discipline. However, before you start cutting, I suggest you read the section on published and unpublished vehicles.

Quality. The quality of your humor must be high in terms of content, appropriateness, and funniness. Since there will be critics in your field waiting to assault your material as feeble and pathetic attempts at humor, be certain that the humorous material you choose is clever, strategically placed, and hysterical. Field testing your humor with different levels of testees similar to the process used to try out other forms of humor is essential (see Chapters 3 and 5). Ask colleagues and friends to read your work before submitting it for publication. There is a major distinction between the humor you present and the humor in print. A joke that bombs in class or in a presentation can be discarded or revised for future use. Its life may be only a few fleeting moments, but written humor is forever. It cannot be changed. Face it, it's in concrete, especially if it was published in an article or a book. The reputation you receive from those jokes will follow you everywhere, into your classes, committee meetings, conferences, garage sales, bus stations, and even encounters with "time-share" representatives who will lock you in a small dingy room with one light bulb dangling from a string and threaten your family until you break down and buy a week no one else wants, after which you all get gift T-shirts made in Malaysia. Although some of your humor may come back to haunt you, the initial investment in the quality of your work will pay dividends in satisfaction and, who knows, maybe buckets of money so you can buy the Caribbean island you've always wanted.

Quantity. The distribution of humor throughout a written document needs to be evaluated not only for where it appears, but also for the amount. Too much humor can be distracting in a serious research paper. The problem is that once you've shifted gears into "humor mode," it is easy to go overboard. In your zeal to integrate humor, you may tend to err in the direction of quantity instead of quality, as I keep doing repeatedly through this book. I may insert some sidebar I think is clever, but it just isn't funny. The quality can be diminished quickly, as you have probably noticed.

Thong 2: Published and Unpublished Vehicles for Humor

The preceding factors ultimately govern whether your efforts to incorporate humor are warranted. If you can expect rejection of your submission because of the humor, then don't even consider it. Reviewers will be unmercifully clear in their opinions on the appropriateness of the humor. When in doubt, don't do it. Although such setbacks can stunt your growth (usually your height, but not necessarily your width) as a humorist by thwarting your humor skills and humorous spirit, it is best to direct those energies toward print sources with editors and readers who are tolerant and maybe even appreciative. In order to send you on a constructive course, I have subthonged this section into "high-probability vehicles" and "low-probability road blocks" for using humor. (Now you knew sooner or later, given my background, that "probability" language would be introduced; after all, I waited until this chapter. Do you have any idea how hard it was to restrain myself from statistical compulsions for seven chapters?) (How's that for an irrelevant and unfunny sidebar?). The suggestions that follow are based on my own experiences in education, psychology, and healthcare. They may not generalize to your discipline. However, it is easy enough to test the waters or other fluids.

High-Probability Vehicles. There are a few outlets for your humor that have a high probability of acceptance: (a) papers presented at regional, national, and international conferences, (b) chapters in conference proceedings or books which were originally keynote, plenary, or other types of invited addresses, (c) articles in journals that specialize in publishing humor, and (d) textbooks and topical volumes in your discipline.

Most professional conferences that use a peer review process to determine acceptance or rejection of papers usually require a detailed proposal or abstract. Although what you submit for this review many months before the conference may contain absolutely super-serious content, (*Note:* Sorry for interrupting this sentence, but I just wanted to say, "Here comes the sneaky part") the final full-length paper doesn't have to. Acceptance of the "what" does not include any decision on "how" it will be presented. You can experiment with any of the preceding humor techniques in your paper and delivery.

There are three risks you need to consider in that presentation: (1) the audience's receptivity or rejection of your humor, (2) the critics' or discussants' reaction, and (3) whether you can scrape together enough dough to get to your presentation to be insulted. This last risk really isn't a risk; it's more of an obstacle. But my pet pot-bellied pig, called Babe (named after that cute little movie star, Beethoven), oinked all night long until I assured him I would add (3) to the list. Assuming you are able to conquer this obstacle, the greatest risk is the possible embarrassment by the discussants. Their remarks about your paper may be biased by your use of humor or they may comment on the "inappropriateness" of the humor itself. If the discussants are assigned to sessions prior to the conference and you know who they are, their reputation could guide your decision about your use of humor. You could also talk with them about the humor to detect their reactions in advance. In regard to your audience's reaction, if your choice of humor satisfies the criteria cited *ad nauseum* (Latin for "this ad makes me puke") throughout this book, they will probably love it in contrast to all of the deadly presentations they have had to endure at the conference.

When you serve as a discussant to critique several papers, use that opportunity to inject humor in your comments to liven up your presentation. Just be careful not to put down the authors or their contributions. The critique of their substantive work should be tactfully executed, not expressed in the form of the "butt" of a joke.

Invited addresses at professional conferences are frequently recorded and transcribed or the authors are requested to submit complete papers of their addresses to the organizers. These papers may then be edited and assembled into a conference proceedings or edited book. Assuming you would now take advantage of the suggestions in Chapter 7 to incorporate humor in your address, pick some of the best material for the chapter version. Since the humor was part of the original presentation, it should legitimately be included in your written product of the conference. In fact, you can add, delete, and/or revise anything in the chapter before it goes to press, so why not modify the humor as well as the substance. I have never had any difficulties retaining the humor in the final published version. The invited presentation provides an excellent opportunity to write and deliver a variety of humorous material and then to transform the most effective material into written form for publication in a chapter.

Beyond this publication outlet for your humor, there are particular journals that specialize in the publication of humorous articles which have no scholarly merit whatsoever. The two most widely known are the *Journal of Polymorphous Perversity* and *The Annals of Improbable Research* (formerly *The Journal of Irreproducible Results*). If you really enjoy writing humorous articles with no redeeming scientific value as I do, then you need to consider these journals. Their editors along with other humorous journals, magazines, and newsletters are listed in Table 2 (Chapter 4).

If you're reeelly serious about your humor, then you might want to invest in writing a textbook, which is the only suggestion here that has any potential for significant financial returns on your use of humor. Depending on your discipline and the undergraduate or graduate level focus of the book, review all of the forms of humor described in this book to determine which ones seem appropriate for the subject matter. One of the most versatile forms employed in the statistics books mentioned previously (Norman & Streiner, 1994, 1997) is the use of humorous examples and illustrations. That form alone will probably distinguish your text from all others in your field. (*Personal Note:* I have toyed with the idea of writing a humorous statistics or measurement text for quite some time, but I have hesitated because I don't know anything about either of those subjects, plus there are some other considerations that lead us smoothly into the next paragraph. Read on, Desdemona.)

Before pursuing a humorous textbook venture, evaluate the book's salability. Although students may love it, it may never see the dim digestive-enzyme green fluorescent light of your college bookstore if professors refuse to use it or to recommend it because they perceive it as a joke, unprofessional, sick and perverted, or demeaning to their discipline or profession. Be realistic about how such a volume would be received by your peers and even how it could affect your credibility. Less ambitious projects, such as smaller humor books on specific topics, edited works on humor in your field (which could be really small), or a humorous psychic-diet abs-of-steel washboard-buns guidebook, may be worth considering to test the market for humor. (*Paragraphus Interruptus:* Speaking of infomercials, one of my favorites is the one where a highly-paid studio audience cheers wildly when they see a spaghetti sauce stain removed from a dress. Maybe it's just me, but I don't think that's as amazing as, for example, seeing a sheep dog covered in motor oil transformed into a Stealth bomber or a pair of Dockers. That's something to rave about. Now back to the last line of this section.) Several of these types of books have been published in medicine and nursing (see Chapter 4).

Low-Probability Road Blocks. There are three categories of publications and reports where the use of humor is usually judged as inappropriate: (a) articles in scholarly, research, and practitioner-oriented journals, (b) chapters in edited volumes, other than proceedings, and (c) research proposals, reports, and critiques/reviews for government agencies and private research institutes and corporations.

> **WARNING:** This next paragraph contains graphic language about organs and self-inflicted violence in a peaceful, though tastefully decorated, office setting. If the paragraph were acted out on TV, it would be rated TV-P30 for professors thirtysomething or older who have previously witnessed office violence. If you are prone to getting upset over these descriptions, you might want to get some Mylanta or Yourlanta to keep at your side. If you want to do that now, I'll wait; unless of course, you have to drive to the pharmacy. It's probably a good idea, because if you think this paragraph could be disturbing, wait until you read the next page.

One's worst fears of rejection by editors and reviewers for professional journals can be easily realized when you incorporate humor into your article. If your substantive contribution is worth publishing, you can end up shooting yourself in one or more kidneys when humorous material is included. A typical response by an editor might be: "It [the humor] is offensive in a professional publication intended to communicate substantive knowledge, plus your kidney is leaking all over my astroturf carpet. Please put your Uzi away." My hit rate with journals in my field is abysmal. To give you a flavor and mouth fungus of how editors and reviewers of blind, refereed journals respond to humor-infested manuscripts, here is a sampling of "real" comments I have received to papers I submitted that contained colorful language, graphic metaphors, cautions and warnings, lots of sidebars, top 10 lists, and/or multiple-choice jokes:

- "If you remove all of your "colorful" language and attempts at humor ... and are willing to follow through with the suggestions we indicate, we would be very interested in publishing the resulting manuscript."

- "Although this manuscript was cleverly written and somewhat amusing, its basic silliness does not lend itself to publication in the journal."

- "If you rewrite the paper without the use of the metaphor, we would reconsider publication."
- "I found the flippant style gimmicky, distracting, and inappropriate for the journal."
- "It is a well-written breath of fresh air on the topic of 'standards'."
- "It was entertaining reading, but it was more suited to *Chicago Hope Magazine* than the journal."
- "The author has tried hard to write a spritely piece; what comes across (to me, at least) is a paper that is overly "cute" ... The author will need to change his/her style and attempt a slightly more scholarly presentation."
- "If the article were revised in a more appropriate style, I think it would be worth publishing."
- "While I applaud attempts to bring some levity to the discussions, when something appears in print, there is an even finer line between humor and tastelessness."
- "I think the paper has an extremely clever way of presenting the overview, but that it needs to be toned down (a little)."
- "I fear the article in its current form may present some liabilities to the profession. I would not like to be testifying in a case and have the opposing attorney ask me if I selected the judges by 'digging them up!' One could argue that this criticism is being overly paranoid, but I'd be willing to argue the point."
- "If there is ever a *National Lampoon* issue of the journal, we might reconsider."

Reading this list again induced symptoms of my disabling, chronic disorder, diagnosed as Humor Reflux Syndrome or HRS, named after the physician who discovered it, Dr. Syndrome. It requires that I regularly ingest megadoses of Zantagametamucilicpeplanta. I know. You don't have to remind me. It's time to buck up and get on with this chapter.

When you encounter the type of resistance conveyed by most of these comments in your own discipline, your choices are simple: (1) acquiesce to the editor's and reviewers' recommendations to remove all color and humor if you want the remaining boring content to be published (i.e., the path of least resistance), (2) continue to resubmit to other journals with editorial boards that may be more tolerant, (3) subsidize a "mob-like" vaporization of the editor responsible, or (4) contact Dr. Kevorkian for advice on how to put this gut-wrenching dilemma to rest once and for all (if you get my drift). Essentially, the second choice requires persistence that may produce some personal satisfaction or victory if you succeed, but a lot of frustration and an unpublished manuscript if you don't. I have had several experiences with the first two options and ended up with many more failures than successes with the second choice. My suggestion is to weigh the value of the substantive contribution the article would make to the field against the disappointment of having to cut everything out of the article that made it more interesting and fun to read.

Using humor in chapters you are requested to write for edited books can be met with the same responses listed previously. Many book editors, who could be professors you have not even met, typically have the sense of humor of airport security personnel standing at the metal detectors just waiting for their moment of glory to wrestle you to the ground and cuff you like the cops on "Bad Boys, Bad Boys, What Ya Gonna Do." However, even if your editor is basically a whimsical person (which is at the same chance level as the New York Jets winning the Super Bowl), he or she would usually not permit the humor in just your chapter. It alters the style and tone of the whole book, inasmuch as it is inconsistent with all of the other chapters. Further, once the chapters are sent out for peer review, I'll give you a wild guess as to the most likely outcome of the reviewers' comments on the appropriateness of your humor. If the editorial process for the book is similar to that of your professional journals, then you're sunk. You'll need to find another outlet for your humor, such as one of the high-probability vehicles mentioned in the preceding section, or a book like this, where you can make up everything as you go along and not have to bother with stuff like knowledge, research, or canned fruit.

The final road block to humor is the research proposal, report, or review you may be asked to prepare for a government agency at any level or private research corporation. These institutions mean serious business. (I really don't want to write this paragraph. I'm already gagging. Seriously.) Although humor may be acceptable and possibly appreciated at meetings with representatives from the various agencies, any form of humor in the written documents you are being paid to submit is inappropriate. Don't even think about it.

Thong 3: Humor in Academic Communications and Documents
Conservation of forests, amber waves, grain, and purple majesties does not seem to be a priority in institutions of higher education. There is an excessive amount of paper pushing and shoving in the forms of memos, agendas, minutes, reports, and parking tickets. Computers have barely made a dent in reducing the avalanche of paper that's burying everyone. It's probably not that different in other bureaucracies.

Since written documents are indigenous to our institutions, as a budding humorist you should be able to take advantage of that phenomenon to have some fun with routine communications. Certainly those communications originating with our superiors must be taken seriously. However, the information received may not necessarily require a serious response. If you are thinking humorously, which I certainly hope you are by now, watch carefully for documents that you generate or respond to that may be appropriate vehicles for humor. The operative word here is "appropriate." Consider the consequences of using the humor. There may be some faculty and administrators who will appreciate your jocular efforts, but there are always others who WON'T. This section examines a few ideas for injecting humor into three types of standard written and electronic communications and documents that you prepare: (a) correspondence, (b) meeting agendas and minutes, and (c) committee reports. These ideas are also applicable to the business communications and meetings of professional associations.

Correspondence. Most office correspondence tends to be either information items or requests for a response. Serving in the role of chairperson or member of a committee, department head, or professor, seize every opportunity (or *carpe tunis casserolus*) to incorporate humor into any form of correspondence you send to colleagues. Draw on every technique described in this book to "jocularize" relatively innocuous memos, letters, and e-mail. Write fake memos that are parodies of departmental and university policies, rules, and procedures, such as annual and sick leave, travel guidelines, reimbursement for travel expenses, letters of recommendation, warning letters, parking regulations, and the standardized format for vitae. Since the content of every memo is different, there is no formula I can suggest to guide your humorous thoughts. When you respond to correspondence from deans and faculty, use humor only if it is appropriate and timely, and you know the recipients will appreciate it.

Meeting Agendas and Minutes. The agenda you prepare for a meeting could be the most structured and prosaic document you write. (The minutes probably would rank second.) It emits boredom and listlessness, but it also cries out: "Pump some life into me; give me a dose of funniness." (*Note:* Not all agendas cry out the same way, although the spirit of their cry for life is usually quite similar.) It is the agenda's structure and predictability that render it amenable to humor.

Every agenda has a title, introduction, body, and ending. By now you know what type of expression you can stick under the title, one that hits you like a bug splattering on your windshield. For example, "A THIRD LESS CONTENT, SAME GREAT TASTE!" might work. Splat! Modifying the introduction and ending to reflect the pomp and circumstance of a professional sports event, such as the Olympics, is one method to create an unexpected twist:

1. Opening Ceremonies
    a. Sing: *Star Spangled Banner* and *God Bless America*
    b. Welcome: (<u>chairperson</u>) (Hum *Hail to the Chief*)
    c. Light the Research Flame (Symbolizing our freedom to burn money; lots of it!)
2. Approval of minutes taken and hours lost
3. (Body of Agenda)
4. Closing Ceremonies
    a. Awards Presentation: Pride, Envy, Sloth, etc.
    b. Sing: *God Save the Queen*
    c. Extinguish Research Flame (Pour large data set over it to smother)

These components can be adapted to almost any agenda. In fact, when I receive an agenda from a colleague, I will revise it and distribute it at the meeting as "REVISED: NEW and IMPROVED." Of course, I can only get away with that with certain colleagues.

The body of the agenda is usually content specific and, as such, requires more imagination to put a humorous spin on each line. If you are the chair, responsible for assembling the agenda items, I encourage you to give it a shot. If not, it's best not to tamper with someone else's body (agenda, that is).

All of the preceding suggestions for transforming a dull agenda into a jocular masterpiece are applicable to the report of meeting minutes. Once you are asked to take the minutes and then distribute your version with opening and closing ceremonies at the meeting, you may never be honored with that task again. Invoking your twistedness in a document as sacred as "minutes" can easily discredit your contributions. Depending on your professional goals, this could be a boon or bane to your committee workload.

Committee Reports. View a committee report as an opportunity to field test humorous material you plan to use in class, professional presentations, and articles. Utilize the techniques mentioned at the beginning of this chapter as well as any other gimmicks you can create in both the written report and your "presentation" of that report. Be sensitive to the composition of the committee in terms of whether the members are humor friendly. Also, consider the timing and appropriateness of your humor. If the overall mood, level of tension, and "affect" indicate that the humor may not be well-received, don't do it. There are some meetings where the Critical Faculty Mass is clearly not conducive to any form of jocularity. If you attempt humor in your committee report under those conditions, not only are you at a high risk of dying (as in bombing), but also at that same risk level of being killed (as in murdered) by the committee.

A final note regarding the preparation of humorous reports and minutes: If these documents are placed in department files that may be reviewed by outsiders in the future for accreditation of programs or other purposes, develop separate humorless versions for those files. The appreciation of your humor within your department or school may not be generalizable to outside consultants and reviewers. Given the ease with which humor can be misunderstood and misinterpreted, it can just as easily result in a loss of your professional credibility. Furthermore, the negative consequences can extend to your colleagues and the reputation of your department, which may tolerate (or even encourage) such inappropriate pathetic displays of silliness. Your efforts to make work fun should never be promoted at the expense of your colleagues or institution.

References

Abrahams, M. (Ed.). (1993). *More of the best of the Journal of Irreproductible Results: Sex as a heap of malfunctioning rubble.* New York: Workman Publishing.

Adams, W. J. (1974). The use of sexual humor in teaching human sexuality at the university level. *Family Coordinator, 23,* 365–368.

Allen, S. (1986). *How to make a speech.* New York: McGraw-Hill.

Allen, S. (1987). *How to be funny: Discovering the comic in you.* New York: McGraw-Hill.

Allen, W. (1971). *Getting even.* New York: Vintage Books.

Allen, W. (1975). *Without feathers.* New York: Random House.

Allen, W. (1980). *Side effects.* New York: Ballantine Books.

Andrews, B. L. (1994). *Digging your own grave.* New York: St. Martin's Press.

Asimov, I. (1971). *Isaac Asimov's treasury of humor.* Boston: Houghton Miffin.

Barry, D. (1988). *Dave Barry's greatest hits.* New York: Fawcett Columbine (Ballantine Books).

Barry, D. (1989). *Dave Barry slept here.* New York: Fawcett Columbine (Ballantine Books).

Barry, D. (1991). *Dave Barry talks back.* New York: Crown Publishers.

Barry, D. (1994). *Dave Barry is not making this up.* New York: Fawcett Columbine (Ballantine Books).

Beard, H., & Cerf, C. (1994). *The official politically correct dictionary and handbook.* New York: Villard Books.

Bell, A., Favale, V., & Kolin, D. (1996). *Comedy Central presents web sightings: A collection of web sites we'd like to see.* New York: Pocket Books.

Berk, L. S., Tan, S. A., Nehlsen-Cannarella, S., Napier, B. J., Lewis, J. E., Lee, J. W., & Eby, W. C. (1988). Humor associated laughter decreases cortisol and increases spontaneous lymphocyte blastogenesis. *Clinical Research, 36,* 435A.

Berk, L. S., Tan, S. A., Napier, B. J., & Eby, W. C. (1989a). Eustress of mirthful laughter modifies natural killer cell activity. *Clinical Research, 37,* 115A.

Berk, L. S., Tan, S. A., Fry, W. F., Jr., Napier, B. J., Lee, J., W., Hubbard, R. W., & Lewis, J. E. (1989b). Neuroendocrine and stress hormone changes during mirthful laughter. *American Journal of the Medical Sciences, 298* (December), 390–396.

Berk, R. A. (1997a). Student ratings of 10 strategies for using humor in college teaching. *Journal on Excellence in College Teaching.*

Berk, R. A. (1997b). Top 10 strategies for using humor as an effective teaching tool. In J. A. Chambers (Ed.), *Selected papers from the Eighth National Conference on College Teaching and Learning* (pp. 9–27). Jacksonville, FL: Center for the Advancement of Teaching and Learning, Florida Community College.

Berk, R. A., & Nanda, J. P. (1997). Effects of jocular instructional methods on attitudes, anxiety, and achievement in statistics courses. *HUMOR: International Journal of Humor Research.*

Berko, I. M., & Bonzo, U. R. (1996). Jocular Scale of Whimsical Frivolity: A boring analysis of really fun data. *Journal of Rejected Manuscripts No One Else Will Publish, 1,* 98634–98644.

Bland, H., Falzarano, P., Niles, B., & Sears, M. (1993). *Life is too short.* New York: Warner Books.

Block, A. (1991). *The complete Murphy's Law: A definitive collection.* Los Angeles: Price Stern Sloan.

Blumenfeld, E., & Alpern, L. (1994). *Humor at work.* Atlanta: Peachtree Publishers.

Booher, D. (1974). *Communicate with confidence!* New York: McGraw-Hill.

Browning, R. (1977). Why not humor? *APA Monitor, 1,* 32.

Bryant, J., Brown, D., Silberberg, A., & Elliott, S. (1981). Effects of humorous illustrations in college textbooks. *Human Communication Research, 8,* 43–57.

Bryant, J., Comisky, P. W., & Zillmann, D. (1979). Teacher's humor in the college classroom. *Communication Education, 28,* 110–118.

Bryant, J., Crane, J. S., Comisky, P. W., & Zillmann, D. (1980a). Relationship between college teachers' use of humor in the classroom and students' evaluations of their teachers. *Journal of Educational Psychology, 72,* 511–519.

Bryant, J., Gula, J. M., & Zillmann, D. (1980b). Humor in communication textbooks. *Communication Education, 29,* 125–134.

Capehart, M. R. (1976). A suggestoaedia-based strategy for teaching statistics to mathophobic college students. *Journal of Suggestive-Accelerative Learning and Teaching, 1,* 164–181.

Carter, J. (1989). *Stand-up comedy: The book.* New York: Dell.

Charney, M. (1995). Woody Allen's non sequiturs. *HUMOR: International Journal of Humor Research, 8,* 339–348.

Cornett, C. E. (1986). *Learning through laughter: Humor in the classroom.* Bloomington, IN: Phi Delta Kappa Educational Foundation.

Cousins, N. (1989). *Head first: The biology of hope and the healing power of the human spirit.* New York: Penguin Books.

Dane, C. S. (1992). *Life's little destruction book: A parody.* New York: St. Martin's Press.

Dane, C. S. (1993). *More Life's little destruction book: A parody.* New York: St. Martin's Press.

Darling, A. L., & Civikly, J. M. (1987). The effect of teacher humor on student perceptions of classroom communicative climate. *Journal of Classroom Interaction, 22*(1), 24–30.

Davis, J. (1991). *Not the SAT.* New York: Dell Publishing.

Davis, K. (1991). *Secrets of dynamic communication: Preparing and delivering powerful speeches.* Grand Rapids, MI: Zondervan.

Detz, J. (1992). *How to write and give a speech.* New York: St. Martin's Press

Dillon, K., Minchoff, B., & Baker, K. (1985). Positive emotional states and the enhancement of the immune system. *International Journal of Psychiatry in Medicine, 15* (January), 13–17.

Edwards, C. M., & Gibboney, E. R. (1992). *The power of humor in the college classroom.* Paper presented at the annual meeting of the Western States Communication Association, Boise, ID.

Ehrlich, H. (1992). *Writing effective speeches*. New York: Paragon House.

Ellenbogen, G. C. (Ed.). (1989). *The primal whimper: More readings from the Journal of Polymorphous Perversity*. New York: Ballantine Books.

Elmore, P. B., & Pohlmann, J. T. (1978). Effects of teacher, student, and class characteristics on the evaluation of college instructors. *Journal of Educational Psychology, 70,* 187–192.

Filson, B. (1991). *Executive speeches: 51 CEOs tell you how to do yours*. Williamstown, MA: Williamstown Publishing.

Flacks, N., & Rasberry, R. W. (1982). *Power talk: How to use theater techniques to win your audience*. New York: The Free Press.

Flynn, L. B. (1960). *Serve Him with joy*. Wheaton, IL: Key Publishers.

Frankel, K., Wilson, R., & Salo, B. (1996). *Off the wall: The best graffiti off the walls of America*. Atlanta: Longstreet Press.

Fry, W. F., Jr. (1971). Mirth and oxygen saturation levels of peripheral blood. *Psychotherapy and Psychosomatics, 19*(1), 76–84.

Fry, W. F., Jr. (1984a). Laughter and health. *Encyclopedia britannica, medical and health annuals: Special report* (pp. 259–262). Chicago: Encyclopedia Britannica.

Fry, W. F., Jr. (1984b, June). *Learning with humor*. Paper presented at the annual meeting of the International Conference on Humor, Tel Aviv, Israel.

Fry, W. F., Jr. (1986). Humor, physiology, and the aging process. In L. Nahemow, K. A. McCluskey-Fawcett, & P. E. McGhee (Eds.), *Humor and aging* (pp. 81–98). Orlando, FL: Academic Press.

Fry, W. F., Jr. (1992). The physiological effects of humor, mirth, and laughter. *Journal of the American Medical Association, 267*(4), 1857–1858.

Fry, W. F., Jr., & Rader, C. (1977). The respiratory components of mirthful laughter. *Journal of Biological Psychology, 19,* 39–50.

Fry, W. F., Jr., & Savin, W. M. (1988). Mirthful laughter and blood pressure. *HUMOR: International Journal of Humor Research, 1,* 49–62.

Fry, W. J., Jr. & Stoft, P. E. (1971). Mirth and oxygen saturation levels of peripheral blood. *Psychotherapy and Psychosomatics, 19,* 76–84.

Gallagher, I. A. (1997). Smashing inanimate objects that ooze and squirt: New uses for leftovers. In M. Stewart, *Food in your face* (pp. 123–147). Hellodeli, NY: Sledgehammer Press.

Geisel, T. S., & Geisel, A. S. (1990). *Oh, the places you'll go! By Dr. Seuss*. New York: Random House.

Gonick, L., & Smith, W. (1993). *The cartoon guide to statistics*. New York: Harper Perennial.

Goodman, J. (1995). *Laffirmations: 1001 Ways to add humor to your life and work.* Deerfield Beach, FL: Health Communications.

Greene, M., Benton, P., Carter, J., & Ross, D. (1997). Physiological benefits of mirth in the ER: A few random observations. *JOCULAR: Journal of Ocular Sightings that Seemed Funny at the Time, 3,* 47–49.

Gruner, C. R. (1967). Effects of humor on speaker ethos and audience information gain. *Journal of Communication, 17,* 228–233.

Gruner, C. R. (1970). The effect of humor in dull and interesting informative speeches. *Central States Speech Journal, 21,* 160–166.

Hamlin, S. (1988). *How to talk so people listen.* New York: Harper & Row.

Hashem, M. E. (1994). *Play and humor in the college classrooom: Using play as a teaching teachnique in interpersonal communication classes.* Paper presented at the annual meeting of the Central States Communication Association, Oklahoma City.

Helitzer, M. (1993). *Comedy writing secrets.* Cincinnati: Writer's Digest Books.

Hoff, R. (1992). *"I can see you naked."* Kansas City, MO: Andrews and McMeel.

Iapoce, M. (1988). *A funny thing happened on the way to the board room: Using humor in business speaking.* New York: Wiley.

Kaplan, R. M., & Pascoe, G. C. (1977). Humorous lectures and humorous examples: Some effects upon comprehension and retention. *Journal of Educational Psychology, 69,* 61–65.

Kipfer, B. A., & Strnad, E. (1996). *The optimist's/pessimist's guide to the millennium.* New York: Perigee Book (Berkley Publishing).

Klein, D. M., Bryant, J., & Zillmann, D. (1982). Relationship between humor in introductory textbooks and student's evaluations of the tests' appeal and effectiveness. *Psychological Reports, 50,* 235–241.

Korobkin, D. (1988). Humor in the classroom: Considerations and strategies. *College Teaching, 26(4),* 154–158.

Kuhn, C. C. (1994). The stages of laughter. *Journal of Nursing Jocularity, 4(2),* 34–35.

Larsen, M. C. (1995). *Oddball sayings, witty expressions, and down home folklore: A collection of clever phrases.* San Jose, CA: R & E Publishers.

Letterman, D., et al. (1990). *The "late night with David Letterman" book of top ten lists.* New York: Pocket Books.

Letterman, D., et al. (1991). *An altogether new book of top ten lists.* New York: Pocket Books.

Letterman, D., et al. (1995). *David Letterman's book of top ten lists and zesty lo-cal chicken recipes.* New York: Bantam Books.

Letterman, D., et al. (1996). *David Letterman's new book of top ten lists and wedding dress patterns for the husky bride.* New York: Bantam Books.

Lloyd, E. L. (1938). The respiratory mechanism in laughter. *Journal of General Psychology, 10,* 179–189.

Magadatz, J. (1993). *1001 Ways NOT to be romantic.* Naperville, IL: Casanova Press.

Malloy, M. (1996). *Semi-deep thoughts.* New York: Pinnacle Books (Kensington Publishing).

Martin, R. A., & Dobbin, J. P. (1988). Sense of humor, hassles, and immunoglobulin A: Evidence for a stress-moderating effect of humor. *International Journal of Psychiatry in Medicine, 18,* 93–105.

Martin, R. A., & Lefcourt, H. M. (1983). The sense of humor as a moderator of the relationship between stressors and mood. *Journal of Personality and Social Psychology, 45,* 1313–1324.

Martin, R. A., & Lefcourt, H. M. (1984). Situational Humor Response Questionnaire: A quantitative measure of the sense of humor. *Journal of Personality and Social Psychology, 47,* 145–155.

Mayer, D. (Ed.). (1996). *Cyber jokes: The funniest stuff on the internet.* Kansas City, MO: Andrews and McMeel.

McMorris, R. F., Boothroyd, R. A., & Pietrangelo, D. J. (1997). Humor in educational testing: A review and discussion. *Applied Measurement in Education, 10,* 269–297.

McTigue, G. G. (1994). *You know you're middle-aged when...* New York: Pinnacle Books (Windsor Publishing).

Mehrens, W. A., & Lehmann, I. J. (1991). *Measurement and evaluation in education and psychology* (4th ed.). Fort Worth, TX: Harcourt Brace Jovanovich.

Montgomery, R. L. (1979). *A master guide to public speaking.* New York: Harper & Row.

Moses, N. W., & Friedman, M. M. (1986). Using humor in evaluating student performance. *Journal of Nursing Education, 25*(8), 328–333.

Norman, G. R., & Streiner, D. L. (1994). *Biostatistics. The bare essentials.* St. Louis: Mosby.

Norman, G. R., & Streiner, D. L. (1997). *PDQ statistics* (2nd. ed.). St. Louis: Mosby.

O'Brien, T. (1995). *?* Newbury Park, CA: CCC Publications.

Parrott, T. E. (1994). Humor as a teaching strategy. *Nurse Educator, 19*(3), 36–38.

Paskind, H. A. (1932). Effects of laughter on muscle tone. *Archives of Neurological Psychiatry, 28,* 623–628.

Perret, G. (1982a). *Comedy writing step by step*. New York: Samuel French.

Perret, G. (1982b). *How to write and sell your sense of humor.* Cincinnati, OH: Writer's Digest Books.

Perrett, G. (1990). *Comedy writing workbook*. New York: Sterling Publishing.

Perret, G. (1993). *Successful stand-up comedy.* Hollywood, CA: Samuel French Trade.

Powell, J. P., & Andresen, L. W. (1985). Humor and teaching in higher education. *Studies in Higher Education, 10*(1), 79–90.

Scherr, G. H. (Ed.). (1983). *The best of the Journal of Irreproductible Results.* New York: Workman Publishing.

Sigband, N. B., & Bell, A. H. (1994). *Communication for managers* (6th ed.). Cincinnati, OH: South-Western Publishing.

Smith, R. E., Ascough, J. C., Ettinger, R. F., & Nelson, D. A. (1971). Humor, anxiety, and task performance. *Journal of Personality and Social Psychology, 19,* 243–246.

Svebak, S. (1974). Revised Questionnaire of the Sense of Humor. *Scandinavian Journal of Psychology, 15,* 328–331.

Taylor, P. M. (1964). The effectiveness of humor in informative speeches. *Central States Speech Journal, 15,* 295–296.

Trebek, A., & Barsocchini, P. (1990). *The Jeopardy! book.* New York: Harper Perennial.

Trebek, A., & Griffin, M. (1992). *The Jeopardy! challenge.* New York: Harper Perennial.

UCLA Higher Education Research Institute. (1997). *The American freshman: National norms for fall 1996.* Los Angeles: American Council on Education and UCLA Higher Education Research Institute.

Waldoks, M. (Ed). (1994). *The best American humor 1994.* New York: Touchstone (Simon & Schuster).

Warlock, A. (1990). *250 Funniest office jokes, memos, and cartoon pin-ups.* Collinsville, IL: Knightraven Books.

Warlock, A. (1995). *250 Funniest office jokes, memos, and cartoon pinups (Vol. 2).* Collinsville, IL: Knightraven Books.

Watson, M. J., & Emerson, S. (1988). Facilitate learning with humor. *Journal of Nursing Education, 27*(2), 89–90.

Welker, W. A. (1977). Humor in education: Foundations for wholesome living. *College Student Journal Monographs, 11*(2), 252–254.

Whaley, B. (1992). *Why the South lost the war ... and other things I don't understand.* Nashville, TN: Rutledge Hill Press.

Wright, R., & Wright, L. R. (1985). *500 Clean jokes and humorous stories and how to tell them.* Westwood, NJ: Barbour Books.

Zillmann, D., & Bryant, J. (1983). Uses and effects of humor on educational ventures. In P. E. McGhee & J. H. Goldstein (Eds.), *Handbook of humor research* (Vol. II, Applied Studies, pp. 173–193). New York: Springer-Verlag.

Index